How To Catch Smallmouth Bass

MINNETONKA, MINNESOTA

Dick Sternberg honed his smallmouth fishing skills on the wing-dams and backwaters of the Mississippi River. But his love for these explosive fighters has taken him from the shield lakes of Canada to the highland reservoirs of the southern United States.

How To Catch Smallmouth Bass

Printed in 2005.

Tom Carpenter
Director of Book Development

Gina Germ
Photo Editor

Michele Teigen
Senior Book Development Coordinator

Laura Belpedio
Book Development Assistant

Teresa Marrone
Book Production

Principal Photography
Bill Lindner Photography (Bill Lindner, Mike Hehner, Tom Heck, Pete Cozad, Jason Lund)

Additional Photography
Dick Sternberg pp.: 10, 13, 18, 19 both, 20, 24, 30, 31 (3), 35, 37, 39, 43, 45 (3), 53, 55, 71, 131, 133, 153 (2)
©Creative Publishing international pp.: 23, 153
©Jerry Howard/Positive Images p.: 25 (1)
Tom Carpenter/NAFC pp.: 25 (3), 49 all
Joel Young p.: 47 (1)
Lowe Products p.: 68 (lower right)
©Allen Blake Sheldon/Animals, Animals p.: 131

Illustrators
Bill Reynolds pp.: 33 all, 41 all, 81, 93 all, 97, 101 all, 137, 142 both, 147 both, 149, 151
Joe Tomelleri pp.: 11 both, 12 all, 129 all

3 4 5 / 07 06 05

© 2002 North American Fishing Club

ISBN 1-58159-096-2

North American Fishing Club
12301 Whitewater Drive
Minnetonka, MN 55343
www.fishingclub.com

Contents

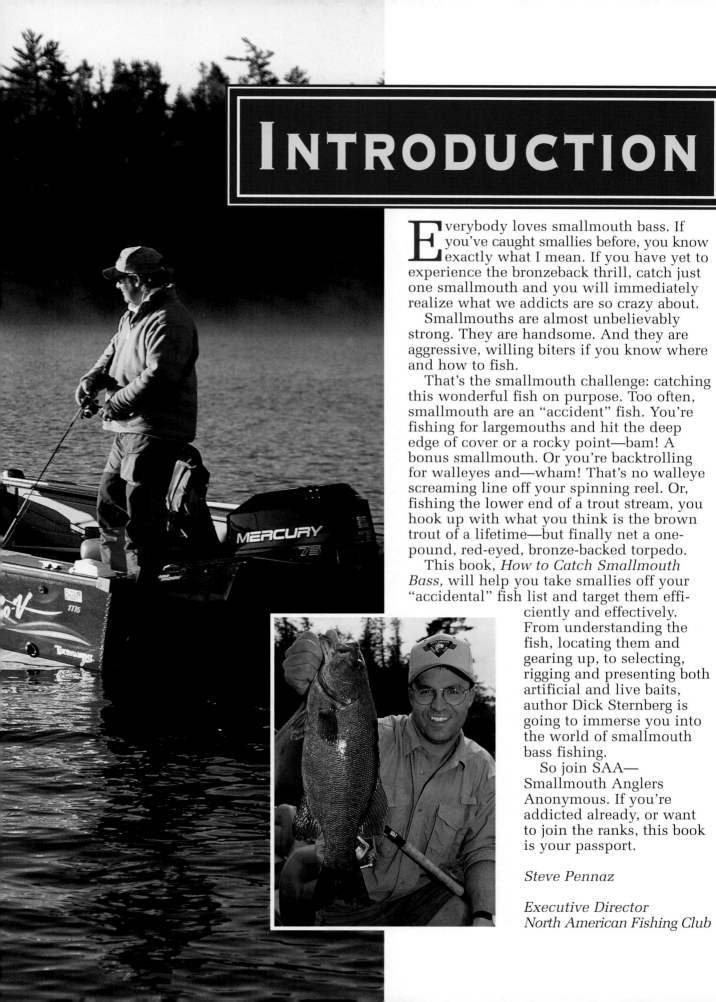

INTRODUCTION

Everybody loves smallmouth bass. If you've caught smallies before, you know exactly what I mean. If you have yet to experience the bronzeback thrill, catch just one smallmouth and you will immediately realize what we addicts are so crazy about.

Smallmouths are almost unbelievably strong. They are handsome. And they are aggressive, willing biters if you know where and how to fish.

That's the smallmouth challenge: catching this wonderful fish on purpose. Too often, smallmouth are an "accident" fish. You're fishing for largemouths and hit the deep edge of cover or a rocky point—bam! A bonus smallmouth. Or you're backtrolling for walleyes and—wham! That's no walleye screaming line off your spinning reel. Or, fishing the lower end of a trout stream, you hook up with what you think is the brown trout of a lifetime—but finally net a one-pound, red-eyed, bronze-backed torpedo.

This book, *How to Catch Smallmouth Bass,* will help you take smallies off your "accidental" fish list and target them efficiently and effectively. From understanding the fish, locating them and gearing up, to selecting, rigging and presenting both artificial and live baits, author Dick Sternberg is going to immerse you into the world of smallmouth bass fishing.

So join SAA— Smallmouth Anglers Anonymous. If you're addicted already, or want to join the ranks, this book is your passport.

Steve Pennaz

Executive Director
North American Fishing Club

5

THE FISH

*B*iologically, smallmouth bass have a lot in common with largemouth, but there are some major differences to consider when planning your fishing strategy.

UNDERSTANDING SMALLMOUTH BASS

Millions of North American anglers place the smallmouth bass on a piscatorial pedestal —and for good reason: Of all the freshwater gamefish, the smallmouth is arguably the gutsiest fighter.

The spectacular fighting ability of the smallmouth is legend. When first hooked, the fish almost always heads right for the surface and makes an explosive leap in an attempt to throw the hook. Often, it succeeds. But if it doesn't, the fish will make several more jumps mixed in with a series of powerful runs that test the skills of any fisherman. This never-give-up determination explains why so many anglers count the smallmouth as their favorite gamefish.

Originally, smallmouth bass were found primarily in the eastern United States with their range extending into the St. Lawrence River drainage in southeastern Canada. But they have been stocked extensively throughout the West and South, and are now found in every state except Florida, Louisiana and Alaska. Self-sustaining populations have also been established in other parts of southern Canada as well as in Hawaii, Asia and even Africa.

Smallmouth bass are close-ly related to largemouth bass and share many of the same waters. But there are some major differences in the habits of the two species (below), and many of those differences have important implications for anglers.

Smallmouth vs. Largemouth

• Smallmouth prefer slightly cooler water than largemouth, explaining why their range does not extend as far south. And when the two species are found in the same body of water, smallmouth are likely to inhabit slightly greater depths.

• As their name suggests, small-mouth have a smaller mouth than largemouth and generally consume smaller food items. This explains why smallmouth anglers use smaller baits than largemouth anglers.

• Wherever crayfish are abundant, they make up a major part of the smallmouth's diet. Largemouth eat crayfish as well, but the crustaceans seldom comprise such a large percentage of the diet. The small-mouth's taste for crayfish may partially explain their preference for rocky structure.

• The smallmouth's penchant for crayfish and various kinds of aquatic insect larvae may also explain its preference for dark- or drab-colored lures. In most waters, a brownish or smoke-colored lure will usually out-produce a lure with bright or gaudy colors. With largemouth, the reverse is generally true.

• It's common for both large-mouth and smallmouth bass to return to the same areas to spawn each spring. But the homing tendency in smallmouth is even stronger than that in largemouth. So if you find a concentration of spawning small-mouth, carefully note the precise location. Chances are they'll be right back in that spot in following years.

• Smallmouth have a more pugnacious, competitive nature than largemouth. It's not uncommon to see several smallmouth chasing another one you've hooked, particularly in waters where food is in short supply. This behavior presents a unique opportunity: When one angler draws in a school of smallmouth, another can drop a lure into the melee and immediately hook another.

Smallmouth are feisty competitors.

SMALLMOUTH BASICS

The smallmouth bass is a member of the sunfish family (*Centrarchidae*), a large and diverse group of fishes sometimes referred to as "centrarchids." All members of the family are warmwater fish and all build nests in which they rear their young. In fact, the name *Centrarchidae* means "nest builders."

Like its close cousin the largemouth, the smallmouth belongs to a group of fishes within the sunfish family called "black bass" (genus *Micropterus*). Other members of the black bass clan include spotted, redeye, Suwannee and Guadalupe bass (p. 12).

Smallmouth are the second-largest member of the group, but reach only about half the maximum size of largemouth.

Smallmouth bass don't really have a small mouth. In fact, it's large compared to that of most other freshwater gamefish. But their mouth is somewhat smaller than that of a largemouth, explaining their name. They're also commonly called bronzebacks, redeyes, brown bass and black bass. The latter name is derived from the color of the fry, which is coal black (p. 23). That fact is also thought to explain the derivation of the group name—black bass.

Taxonomists have identified two subspecies of small-mouth bass: the northern smallmouth (*Micropterus dolomieui dolomieui*) and the Neosho smallmouth (*Micropterus dolomieui velox*). The latter is a stream-dwelling form found primarily in the southern Ozarks. Neosho smallmouth (named for the Neosho River in Missouri) are now quite rare because dams have inundated much of their original stream habitat.

The world-record smallmouth, an 11-pound, 15-ouncer, was caught in Dale Hollow Lake on the Tennessee-Kentucky border in 1955. This long-standing record was recently challenged by a dock worker who claimed he had weighted the fish with 3 pounds of outboard-motor parts soon after the fish had been caught. Based on his unsubstantiated statement, the record was disallowed. However, the dock worker's claims were questioned by several people, including his own brother. After a thorough investigation by the Tennessee Wildlife Resources Agency and The Fresh Water Fishing Hall of Fame, the record was reinstated.

D. L. Hayes still holds the world smallmouth record with this 11-pound, 15-ounce giant. The fish measured 27 inches long and had a 21⅔-inch girth.

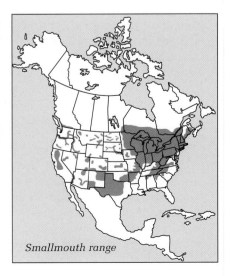

Smallmouth range

Smallmouth Bass Subspecies

Northern Smallmouth

Neosho Smallmouth

Both northern smallmouth (top) and Neosho smallmouth (bottom) are greenish to bronze in color, accounting for the common name, "bronzeback." They have dark vertical bars or diamond patterns on their sides, but these marks are not always present and may come and go. The cheek also has dark bars. The jaw extends to approximately the middle of the eye, which is often reddish. Neosho smallmouth differ slightly from northern smallmouth in that they have a black spot on the rear margin of the gill cover.

Close Relatives of the Smallmouth

Largemouth bass are greenish to tannish in color with a darker back, lighter belly and a dark horizontal band. The jaw is longer than that of the smallmouth, extending past the rear of the eye.

Spotted bass have light greenish sides with a dark lateral band consisting of irregular blotches. The jaw is shorter than that of a largemouth, but longer than that of a smallmouth, extending nearly to the rear of the eye. Each scale below the lateral band may have a distinct dark spot. Spotted bass have a small patch of teeth on their tongue.

Redeye bass get their name from the distinctive reddish eye. The sides and back are brownish with darker blotches. The gill cover has a large black spot and the jaw extends nearly to the rear of the eye. Some redeyes have reddish rear fins, blue spots on the back and sides, and a bluish belly.

Guadalupe bass are generally greenish and have a lateral band consisting of separate dark blotches. They resemble spotted bass in that the scales below the lateral line are spotted, but the Guadalupe's greenish coloration extends much lower on the body. The jaw extends to the rear of the eye.

Suwannee bass are the smallest black bass, seldom exceeding 12 inches in length. The cheeks, breast and belly are bright turquoise. There are a series of dark vertical blotches along the lateral line and a distinct black spot at the base of the tail. The jaw extends to the rear of the eye.

Smallmouth Bass: The Chameleon of Freshwater Fish

Barred smallmouth.

If you're a well-traveled smallmouth angler, you've probably noticed that the fish you take from different bodies of water differ greatly in coloration. Some have a uniform brownish, grayish or greenish color, with practically no barring, while others have an intense bronze background color with distinct dark bars or diamond-shaped marks on the side. And from time to time, you'll catch a smallmouth that is almost pure black.

The reason for this tremendous color variation is the smallmouth's ability to change color to match its surroundings. Only the rock bass rivals the smallmouth as the greatest "chameleon" of North American freshwater fish.

As a rule, smallmouth in murky water have a pale, grayish or greenish coloration, while those from clear water have the typical brownish or bronze color. But even fish from the same body of water can vary greatly in color. For example, a fish roaming open water is likely to be much lighter in color than one holed up under a dock or tucked into a brush pile. In fact, if you catch a dark-colored smallmouth and place it in a white tank, it will lighten up within minutes.

Dark brown smallmouth.

Green smallmouth.

Unusual noises, like those produced by tapping metal tools (above) or rocks, attract curious smallmouth.

SMALLMOUTH SENSES

Any serious smallmouth angler knows that the fish are extremely sight-oriented. In clear lakes, for example, it's possible to "call" smallmouth to the surface from depths of 20 to 30 feet using top-water lures.

More evidence of the smallmouth's visual capability is their penchant for drab or natural-colored lures. While walleyes and northern pike are usually drawn to bright colors, such as chartreuse or red and white, smallmouth show a preference for colors like brown, olive-green and black. In fact, there are times when smallmouth seem alarmed by bright or gaudy lures.

Clearwater smallmouth fishermen know that the fish feed heavily after dark, especially in the summer months. This provides even more evidence of the smallmouth's extraordinary visual capability. In discolored water, however, other senses take over. There, big-bladed spinner-baits, rattlebaits or other lures that produce a definite "beat" or intense vibrations are the best choices.

Many smallmouth anglers favor lures that combine strong vibrations and sound. In muddy water, for instance, a rattlebait (vibrating plug with internal beads) will usually outfish an ordinary vibrating plug with no beads.

Those who doubt that smallmouth respond to sound would quickly change their mind if they donned scuba gear and went down to check it out for themselves. Divers tell of tapping rocks on their air tanks to draw schools of smallmouth to within inches of the commotion.

That type of behavior also reveals another interesting smallmouth trait: curiosity. Smallmouth commonly swim up to inspect a noisy bait, even when they're not interested in feeding.

The sense of smell plays a minimal role in smallmouth fishing. Although some smallmouth fishermen still douse their lures with bottled scent products, many anglers have come to the conclusion that scents don't really provide a noticeable edge and that visual appeal is by far more important.

Anglers in clearwater lakes have discovered that they can "call" smallmouth up to the surface from depths as great as 25 feet using "noisy" lures such as spinnerbaits and minnowbaits.

In low-clarity waters, the extra sound emitted by the shot chamber of a rattlebait may tip the odds in your favor.

Ultra-realistic lures (such as crayfish-imitating crankbaits) work best in clear waters, where smallmouth have plenty of time to inspect your offering.

Bladebaits emit an intense vibration that gets the attention of smallmouth. Even if a smallmouth can't see the lure, the fish can feel the vibrations through its lateral-line system.

FOOD HABITS

When it comes to food, smallmouth bass are opportunists. Their diet varies tremendously from one body of water to another, and even from season to season within the same body of water.

But a review of dozens of food-habit studies reveals one consistent pattern: Wherever crayfish are found in good numbers, they make up a large percentage of the annual food consumption of adult smallmouth—in some cases, more than 75 percent.

Anglers should pay close attention to what smallmouth are eating, because this factor —more than any other— affects their locational patterns and the presentation required to catch them.

Here are some of the more common smallmouth foods along with the feeding patterns normally associated with them:

Crayfish

Ever wonder why smallmouth are so closely linked to rocky bottoms? The main reason is that the rocks hold large numbers of crayfish. But not all rocks make good crayfish habitat. Small boulders or broken rock generally hold more crayfish than unbroken rock outcrops, because they provide more hiding spots. This explains why knowledgeable smallmouth anglers focus on "chunk" rock and avoid "slab" rock.

Although some walleye anglers dislike smallmouth because their populations have boomed in numerous "walleye" lakes, these concerns are overblown. Because smallmouth focus so strongly on crayfish, they are seldom a serious competitive threat to walleyes or, for that matter, other kinds of gamefish with which they commonly share the water.

Where you find shiners, you'll probably find smallmouth as well.

Shiners

Experienced smallmouth fishermen know that shiners have a special appeal to smallmouth bass. In fact, there will be times when smallmouth turn up their noses at fatheads, chubs or other minnows normally available at the local bait shop, but eagerly attack a spottail or emerald shiner. Golden shiners (which are not true shiners) are seldom an important smallmouth food.

Shiners inhabit practically every kind of smallmouth water, but they're most common in sandy, mesotrophic lakes. There, huge schools of shiners invade the shallows to spawn in spring, and the smallmouth are close behind. The best time to find shiners (and smallmouth) in the shallows is on a warm, sunny spring or early-summer day when the water is considerably warmer there than in the depths.

Shad

Threadfin and gizzard shad are common smallmouth foods in rivers and reservoirs throughout the southern two-thirds of the United States, particularly in summer and fall.

Shad hatch in spring and grow rapidly on their plankton diet, usually reaching a size that appeals to smallmouth by midsummer. By late fall, however, they've grown to a length of 6 inches or more, beyond the size that most smallmouth are likely to eat.

In late summer, shad begin to form huge schools in open water as they feed on plankton. One of the most reliable patterns is to play the wind. After a day or two of a steady south wind, for example, clouds of plankton gather along the north shore, drawing large schools of shad which, in turn, attract smallmouth.

At times, smallmouth feed in packs in the same manner as white bass, herding the shad to the surface or into confined bays. But the smallmouth packs are smaller and the action is often short-lived.

Gizzard shad.

Young-of-the-year cisco.

Ciscoes

Ciscoes inhabit tens of thousands of oligotrophic and early- to mid-stage mesotrophic lakes across the northern states and Canada. Cisco-eating smallmouth in northern lakes behave much like shad eaters in southern lakes. Both kinds of baitfish are plankton feeders, meaning that they spend most of their time suspended in open water rather than relating to structure. It's not unusual to see smallmouth pack-feeding on ciscoes, just as they do on shad.

The main difference between the two kinds of baitfish is that ciscoes are coldwater fish, preferring a water temperature in the mid 50s. Shad favor much warmer water, in the mid 70s.

To find temperatures in the mid 50s, ciscoes in northern lakes must descend into the thermocline during the summer months. You're likely to find them at depths of 25 feet or more in midday, although they may feed on or near the surface in the evening or in cloudy weather. It's important to plan your smallmouth fishing according to this locational pattern.

Smelt

These long, thin, silvery baitfish make perfect smallmouth food because they slide down easily and are not likely to lodge in smallmouth's throats.

Although smelt are not as widespread as the other smallmouth foods we've discussed, they're very important in certain waters in the extreme northern U.S. and Canada.

Like ciscoes, smelt are coldwater fish; they're normally found at water temperatures from the low 40s to the mid 50s. But smelt differ from ciscoes in that they feed mainly on small fish (including their own kind) and bottom organisms rather than plankton. This means that smelt are usually found close to the bottom on deep structure.

To find the cold water that they prefer, smelt have to go deep in summer—even deeper than ciscoes. This explains why anglers on northern lakes sometimes catch smallmouth at depths of 40 to 50 feet from late summer into fall.

Rigged smelt.

Insects

In some ways, the feeding habits of smallmouth resemble those of trout. When a heavy insect hatch is in progress, smallmouth forget about crayfish, minnows or whatever else they have been eating and focus on the particular insect that is emerging. During the few days when the hatch is on, that insect is often the only food that smallmouth consume.

In Nebish Lake, Wisconsin, for instance, insects made up 34 percent of the small-mouth's diet in May, when insect hatches were frequent, but only 4 percent in July, after the hatches had subsided. Crayfish were the predominant food item for most of the year, comprising as much as 83 percent of the diet in fall. But they made up only 14 percent of the diet in May, when the fish were focusing on insects.

Smallmouth feed mainly on immature insect forms. When mayfly nymphs emerge from their burrows and slowly wiggle toward the surface to hatch, smallmouth are

Hellgrammite.

there to pick them off. Bass will also root around on a gravelly bottom to dislodge various kinds of nymphs. Once the hatch is underway, smallmouth do not hesitate to slurp the adults off the surface, but the adult forms are available to them for a much shorter time.

When a hatch is in progress, smallmouth often display a strange kind of feeding behavior. They swim around very slowly and methodically, sucking in emerging nymphs and adults struggling on the surface. They ignore most lures and baits, with the exception of flies that resemble the real thing. The most logical explanation for their sluggish demeanor is that they know their prey can't escape, so there is no need to be in a hurry.

Adult mayfly.

Peak Feeding Times

Studies have shown that smallmouth feed most heavily at water temperatures in the upper 70s, and that feeding is virtually nil when temperatures sink into the low 40s.

In a normal year, anglers catch few smallmouth until water temperatures rise into the upper 40s in spring. The action continues to improve as the water warms through the 60s and 70s and feeding activity increases. But when the water temperatures rise into the 80s, feeding slows and so does fishing success. The action picks up again in fall as the water cools, but fades in late fall as temperatures again dip back down into the 40s.

Smallmouth are rarely caught by ice anglers, although ice fishing can be good in lakes with large smallmouth numbers. There, competition for food is great enough to keep the fish biting through the winter months.

GROWTH

As a rule, smallmouth in the southern part of their range grow considerably faster than their counterparts in the northern part, mainly because the growing season in the southern zone is much longer. Because smallmouth feed very little at water temperatures below 40°F, the growing season in the extreme northern part of the range lasts no more than 6 months. In the southern part, it spans practically the entire year.

But that doesn't necessarily mean that southern smallmouths are bigger than their northern relatives. The maximum life span of a smallmouth is much longer in the North—18 years as compared to about 7—so even though a northern smallmouth may grow only half as fast, it may live twice as long, so the end result is not that much different. The largest smallmouth reported from Canada—a 9-pound, 13 ouncer taken in Birchbark Lake, Ontario, in 1954—is only about 2 pounds less than the current world record.

Many other factors affect smallmouth growth, including forage supply, fishing pressure, genetics and size of the body of water in which they live:

Slow-growing smallmouth have a large head compared to the rest of their body.

Fast-growing smallmouth have a small head compared to the rest of their body.

Forage Supply

A shallow, fertile farm-country lake in the North may actually have a greater forage crop than a deep, clear reservoir in the South. So even though the growing season in the latter is much longer, the growth rate of the fish may be similar.

Fishing Pressure

All other factors being equal, a lightly-fished lake will produce bigger smallmouth than one that sees heavy angling pressure. That explains why a deep, cold, infertile Canadian Shield lake in a remote wilderness area may produce numbers of smallmouth in the 5- to 6-pound class, while a fertile but heavily fished lake in a highly populated area kicks out nothing over 2 pounds.

Genetics

While there have been few formal studies on smallmouth bass genetics, there is little doubt that differences in smallmouth growth rates from one body of water to another are a result of differences in the genetic code.

In one moderately fertile central Minnesota lake, for example, numerous smallmouth in the 5- to 7-pound class are taken each year. But in another lake in the same region, the fish rarely exceed 1½ pounds, despite an abundance of baitfish and relatively light fishing pressure.

Size of Water

Smallmouth are prime examples of the "fishbowl effect." Those that live in very small lakes or streams rarely reach a weight of more than a couple of pounds and, in many cases, don't grow large enough to generate much angling interest.

Smallmouth in large bodies of water, on the other hand, are much more likely to grow to trophy size. In fact, some of the best trophy smallmouth fishing in the country can be found in large bays of the Great Lakes, such as Chequamegon Bay on Lake Superior.

The fishbowl effect is also apparent in moving water. It explains why big rivers are much more likely to produce quality smallmouth than smaller streams. In most midwestern smallmouth streams, for example, the fish seldom exceed 2 pounds, while 5-pounders are commonly taken from large rivers in the same region.

Growth Rate of Smallmouth Bass in Various Waters

Body of Water	Length (Inches) at Age in Years												
	1	2	3	4	5	6	7	8	9	10	11	12	13
Massie Creek, Ohio	3.0	5.7	8.5	10.8	12.4	13.8	14.7	15.1					
Des Moines River, Iowa	4.7	9.0	11.7	13.4	15.3	16.2							
Big Piney River, Missouri	3.4	6.3	8.5	10.6	12.8	14.9	16.2	17.1	17.5				
Lake Opeongo, Ontario	2.1	5.2	7.7	9.1	11.1	12.1	13.5	14.5	15.5				
Lake Oneida, New York	3.2	6.0	9.3	11.4	13.1	14.4	14.9	15.6	16.0	16.4	16.8	17.4	17.8
Hog Island, Lake Michigan	4.5	5.9	7.4	8.7	10.5	12.2	14.0	15.6	16.2	17.0	17.7	18.5	
Idlewild Lake, Iowa	2.4	6.0	9.1	12.1	14.3	16.2	18.0	19.4	20.0	20.6			
Pine Flat Lake, California	5.5	8.9	12.5	14.7	16.6	17.9	18.3						
Norris Lake, Tennessee	3.1	8.9	13.3	15.8	17.4	18.0	18.6	20.9					
Pickwick Lake, Alabama	5.9	10.7	13.5	16.6	18.5	20.4	21.0	21.6					
Claytor Lake, Virginia	2.4	6.8	10.9	14.1	17.7	20.4	22.0						

A good-sized boulder makes a male's nest-guarding duties much easier.

SPAWNING HABITS

In spring, when the water temperature reaches the mid- to upper 50s, male smallmouth begin fanning out their nests on a sand, gravel or rubble bottom. More often than not, they'll choose a nesting site alongside a boulder or log; this way, the nest is automatically protected on one side, making it easier to guard the eggs and fry.

Smallmouth can spawn successfully in lakes or streams, but they won't nest in moving water. In big rivers, for example, smallmouth spawn in backwater areas with little or no current. In lakes or streams, you'll normally find the nests in 2 to 4 feet of water. In ultraclear water, however, they've been known to nest in depths of more than 15 feet.

Nesting takes place in the same areas year after year, and there is evidence to show that the fish sometimes use the same nests. But if the water level changes, the fish may have to move a little deeper or shallower to compensate.

Shortly after the males have finished their nest-building chores, females move into the vicinity. Spawning usually begins at water temperatures from 60° to 65°F. In waters that hold both smallmouth and largemouth bass, smallmouth usually spawn a few days earlier and at water temperatures 2 to 4 degrees cooler.

The female deposits her eggs (about 7,000 per pound of body weight) at the same time the male releases his milt. The eggs hatch in 2 to 10 days, depending on the water temperature, and then the male remains to guard the fry until they're large enough to leave the nest.

During the nest-guarding period, which usually lasts about a week, the male is highly aggressive. He will attack anything that comes too close to the nest, including a much larger fish or an angler's lure. The male may stay with some of the fry even after they leave the nest and continue to guard them for up to 2 more weeks.

When first hatched, the fry measure about ⅜ inch in length and are almost completely transparent, with the exception of the black eye and yellowish egg sac (which nourishes them through their first few days of life). But by the time they reach an inch in length, their entire body has started to turn black, giving rise to the term "black bass."

By the end of their first summer, the "fingerlings" are 3 to 5 inches long and have pretty much the same coloration as an adult smallmouth.

Once they reach an inch in length, smallmouth fry (arrow) are almost completely black.

The tail of a smallmouth fingerling has bands of orange and black, with a whitish tip.

Should You Fish for Bedding Smallmouth?

Although most states allow fishing for smallmouth bass during the spawning season, some northern states have a long-standing policy of protecting the fish until spawning has been completed.

But even where catching spawning smallmouth is legal, most responsible anglers immediately release any fish they catch. A preponderance of the smallmouth caught during the spawning period are males and if they are kept, predators will immediately move in and eat the fry. On the other hand, if the males are released unharmed they will quickly return and resume their nest-guarding duties. Anglers have reported catching the same male off the nest several times in a day.

Where there is an abundance of panfish, however, even catch-and-release fishing can be a problem. One fisheries researcher observed a bluegill consume 39 smallmouth fry when the male was driven away for a moment.

Tournament anglers should refrain from targeting nesting smallmouth. Even though the fish are eventually released, they are taken away from the nest, leaving the fry unprotected. In one northern lake popular among tournament anglers, biologists attribute a decline in the smallmouth population to tournament fishing during the nesting period.

Catch-and-release is a vital part of any successful smallmouth-management program.

SMALLMOUTH CONSERVATION

The smallmouth's aggressive nature makes it an easy target for anglers. In heavily fished waters, fishermen can easily overharvest smallmouth, resulting in an abundance of small fish.

To preserve quality angling, many natural resource agencies are now adopting special regulations intended to reduce angler harvest and improve smallmouth size.

For example, on Tennessee's famed Dale Hollow Lake, which produced the world-record smallmouth in 1955, anglers must abide by a 16- to 21-inch "protected" slot limit, with an overall limit of two smallmouth (one under 16 inches and one over 21 inches). On Alabama's Pickwick Lake, anglers must release any smallmouth under 14 inches in length. On Minnesota's Mille Lacs Lake, the smallmouth limit is one fish per day, and it must be over 21 inches in length.

Even where such stringent regulations have not been adopted, there is an ever-increasing movement toward catch-and-release fishing. Although smallmouth are a better-than-average table fish, more and more anglers are recognizing that their spectacular fighting skills make them more valuable in the water than on a dinner plate.

When you release a smallmouth, be sure to handle it gently. Don't let it flop around in the bottom of your boat, and don't grab it by the lower lip and hold it horizontally. Set it back into

Holding a big smallmouth like this may injure its lower jaw.

the water gently rather than tossing it in.

Besides overfishing, smallmouth populations in many parts of the country face a variety of environmental threats as shown on the following page:

Threats to Smallmouth Bass Populations

Overgrazing. *Livestock grazing along a smallmouth stream often causes severe bank erosion, increasing siltation and changing the shape of the channel from deep and narrow to wide and shallow. This means warmer water, lower oxygen levels and fewer spots with sufficient depth.*

Non-Point Pollution. *Root-worm insecticides, other pesticides and herbicides applied to farm fields wash into streams where they are toxic to smallmouth bass, their prey and water quality in general. Many midwestern streams have suffered from this "non-point" pollution arriving from the uplands. Runoff emanating from specific points such as barnyards and feedlots (inset) has also contributed to the habitat degradation.*

Acid Rain. *Acid rain, caused mainly by emissions from coal-burning power plants, has caused the water in some infertile Canadian shield lakes to acidify to the point where smallmouth bass can no longer reproduce. In fact, smallmouth are one of the first species to disappear as a result of acid rain.*

Wetland Drainage. *When wetlands are ditched and drained for agricultural (shown) and other purposes, the intensity of small-stream flooding increases. A heavy spring rain muddies the water when smallmouths are spawning, and severe floods cause siltation of the streambed and wipe out forage species.*

THE WATERS

*B*ecause of their specific habitat needs, smallmouth are easy to find—if you know what to look for.

SMALLMOUTH HABITAT

Fisheries biologists refer to smallmouth bass as an "indicator species" because they are one of the first fish species to disappear when a body of water becomes badly polluted, and one of the first to reappear when the pollution source is removed.

Although smallmouth can survive in a wide range of water types, they are much less adaptable than largemouth bass. As a rule, they prefer clear, clean, cool, well-oxygenated waters. Here are their specific habitat requirements:

Clarity

It's unusual to find a good smallmouth population in waters with a clarity of less than 1 foot, and the best smallmouth waters usually have a clarity of more than 3 feet. Smallmouth can tolerate temporary periods of low clarity from heavy rains or algal blooms, but they rarely thrive in waters that stay murky all year.

Reservoir anglers know that smallmouth are generally most plentiful in the lower reaches of the lake, where the water is clearest. The same principle holds true on many smallmouth streams, where the clearer upper and middle reaches hold more smallmouth than the muddier lower reaches.

Water Temperature

Like its close relative, the largemouth bass, the smallmouth bass is considered a "warmwater" fish. But its preferred temperature range (67 to 71°F) is considerably lower than that of the largemouth (68 to 78°F) and is really closer to that of "coolwater" fish like walleye and northern pike.

Despite its preference for cool water, smallmouth are often found at much warmer temperatures in the heat of summer. That's because the deeper, cooler water in many lakes and reservoirs lacks sufficient dissolved oxygen during the summer months.

Water temperatures below 50°F slow smallmouth feeding considerably and, below temperatures of 40, smallmouth barely feed at all. In a laboratory test, temperatures below 40 caused smallmouth to lie motionless on the bottom and refuse food.

Preferred Habitat of Smallmouth vs. Largemouth Bass

Smallmouth Habitat. *Smallmouth prefer clear, cool water with light to moderate weed growth and a firm gravelly or rocky bottom.*

Largemouth Habitat. *Largemouth thrive in waters of moderate clarity with plenty of weedy or woody cover. They prefer a firm bottom, but will tolerate a softer mud or silt bottom.*

Oxygen Level

Not only do smallmouth need cooler water than largemouth, they require slightly higher oxygen levels. While a largemouth can survive at an oxygen level as low as 2.0 ppm (parts per million), smallmouth require at least 2.5 ppm. This explains why largemouth are found in more fertile or stagnant waters.

But an oxygen level below 5 ppm greatly reduces feeding and growth, meaning that neither species will survive in waters where oxygen levels remain that low for prolonged periods.

Bottom Composition

Most anglers associate smallmouth bass with rocky bottoms. And if a given body of water has rocky or gravelly habitat within the right depth range, that's exactly where you'll find the smallmouth and the best fishing.

There's a good reason why smallmouth prefer a rocky bottom. Insect larvae, crayfish and other invertebrates live beneath the rocks or in the spaces between them, providing smallmouth with a reliable food source. And a rocky or gravelly bottom makes ideal spawning substrate.

But not all rocky bottoms are equal in the eyes of smallmouth. Small or broken rocks are generally better than giant boulders or "slab" rock. Given a choice, smallmouth prefer rocks from softball- to basketball-size.

In lakes where the entire basin is rocky, however, the

Sandy, weedy bays are key smallmouth spots in many lakes with an otherwise rocky basin.

best smallmouth fishing can often be found in sandy, weedy areas. In many Canadian shield lakes, for example, you'll find the biggest smallmouth on sandy humps with plenty of weed growth or in sandy, weedy bays. The weeds evidently attract baitfish which, in turn, draw the smallmouth.

Good Rock vs. Bad Rock

Good rock has plenty of nooks and crannies that serve as cover for a variety of smallmouth foods.

Bad rock is big, and has a smooth, flat surface that is barren of all food organisms.

Depth

In waters that hold both smallmouth and largemouth, you'll generally find the smallmouth in slightly deeper water. But there are no firm rules; like any other predator species, smallmouth go wherever they must to find food.

Throughout most of the year, it's unusual to find smallmouth at depths greater than 30 feet and, more often, they'll be at depths of 20 feet or less. But in some lakes and big rivers, they sometimes form wintering concentrations at depths as great as 60 feet. On large river systems, a certain wintering hole may attract practically all of the smallmouth from many miles of river.

Current Speed

River and stream-dwelling smallmouth prefer current of medium speed, from 0.4 to 1.3 feet per second. That's a little faster than a typical largemouth stream, but a little slower than the average trout stream.

Even though smallmouth favor moderate current, they usually take cover behind a boulder, log or some other object that makes an eddy, so they do not have to keep swimming to maintain their position. This way, they can rest in the slack water and then dart out into the moving water to pick off minnows and other prey.

Many stream fishermen make the mistake of looking for smallmouth in the deepest, slowest-moving pools. But these "holes" are more likely to hold carp, suckers or catfish than smallmouth

A river mouth is an easy source of food for lake-dwelling smallmouth.

bass. Smallmouth prefer a pool with noticeable current.

Current may also be a factor in drawing lake-dwelling smallmouth. For example, smallmouth often concentrate around river mouths or in the narrows between islands, where current attracts large numbers of baitfish.

How to Recognize a Good Smallmouth Stream

The best smallmouth streams have moderate current with plenty of riffles and good-sized pools.

Fast-moving streams with a stair-step configuration and small pools rarely hold good smallmouth populations.

Slow-moving streams with long, flat pools are much better suited to largemouth bass and catfish than to smallmouth bass.

NATURAL LAKES

Smallmouth bass thrive in tens of thousands of natural lakes throughout the northern states and southern Canada. Although they generally reach the highest density in mesotrophic lakes, they're also found in good numbers in some oligotrophic and eutrophic lakes.

"Meso" lakes have enough fertility to produce an abundance of food, but not so much that they "freeze out" in winter because of low oxygen levels. Smallmouth can survive in most any kind of meso lake, but they prefer those with plenty of gravelly or rocky

areas. These features provide spawning habitat and produce crayfish, an abundance of structure, and low populations of competitor species such as largemouth bass and northern pike. Surprisingly, smallmouth can thrive in the face of a large walleye population, and many northcountry lakes offer outstanding fishing for both species.

Although many oligotrophic lakes are too cold and infertile to support smallmouth bass, "oli" lakes toward the higher end of the fertility scale often support excellent smallmouth popula-

tions. And even some of the deepest, coldest oli lakes have warm, shallow sections that are more like meso lakes and hold good numbers of smallmouth.

Most eutrophic lakes are better suited to largemouth than to smallmouth, but some deeper eutrophic lakes with sparse to moderate weed-growth areas and areas of rocky bottom are good smallmouth producers. Because of their abundance of baitfish, eutrophic lakes that can sustain smallmouth often rank among the top trophy waters.

How Various Types of Smallmouth Lakes Differ

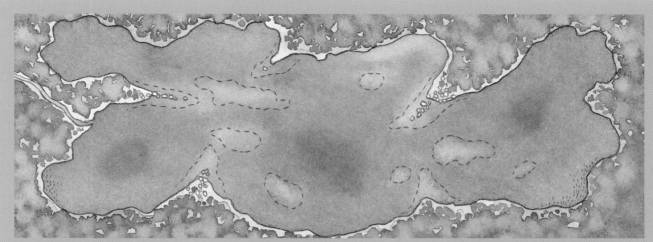

Mesotrophic Lakes. *The best meso lakes have a highly structured basin with plenty of rocky or gravelly humps, points and bars in the shallows, along with some deep wintering holes. Clarity ranges from moderate to high; weed growth, light to moderate.*

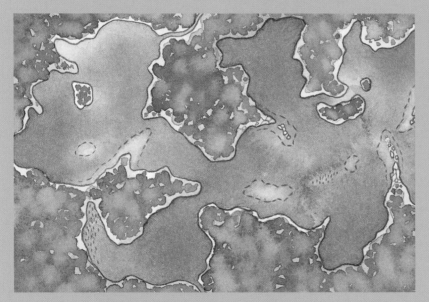

Oligotrophic Lakes. *The ideal oli lake has a gradually sloping shoreline with plenty of mid-lake structure that tops out at 20 feet or less. In addition to the multiple rocky points and humps, there is some sandy, weedy structure as well. Clarity ranges from bog-stained to clear.*

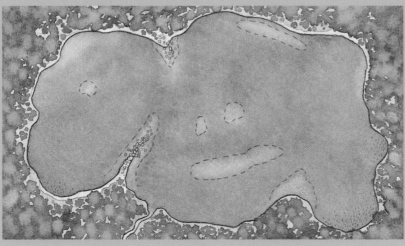

Eutrophic Lakes. *Look for lakes at least 30 feet deep with moderate clarity, light weed growth and gravel bars or rocky humps and points for structure.*

MESO LAKES

Smallmouth anglers who understand the basic seasonal location pattern on meso lakes should have no trouble finding fish in any kind of lake—natural or man-made. Although the type of cover and structure the fish use at various times of the year may differ, the movement principles are exactly the same.

In spring, when the water temperature reaches the mid 40s, smallmouth leave their deep wintering holes and begin moving toward their spawning areas. But long before spawning begins, you'll find them feeding in dark-bottomed bays and on shallow, rocky flats near their spawning areas. There, they find an abundance of minnows and larval insects, especially on warm, sunny days.

Fishing tends to be spotty during this pre-spawn period, because periodic cold fronts drive the fish out of the shallows and slow their feeding activity. But if you hit the weather right, you'll find some spectacular action.

As the water temperature edges into the upper 50s, males begin constructing their nests, usually in sheltered bays, along shorelines protected from the wind or on gradually sloping points, but occasionally on shallow mid-lake humps.

The nests are usually in 2 to 5 feet of water and are rarely deeper than 8, so you should be able to see them on a calm day. Although the nests are often next to a log or boulder, you may find them in beds of emergent vegetation, particularly bulrushes.

Most spawning is completed by the time the water temperature has reached the upper 60s, and the females abandon the nest. But the males remain to guard the eggs and fry for as long as 3 weeks.

By the time the males have finished their nest-guarding duties, the females have recuperated from the rigors of spawning and begin to feed heavily. The next few weeks offer peak smallmouth action. The problem is, the fish are still in transition between their spawning and summertime structure, so locational patterns are not well established. Some fish are still roaming shallow flats in search of baitfish while others are already set up on humps, rock bars and deep points where they will spend the summer.

The next few months offer some of the year's most predictable smallmouth fishing, because you know right where to find the fish. But, with the glut of baitfish that normally becomes available in midsummer, catching them may not be easy. They're a lot fussier than they were in spring, and it may take live bait to draw strikes.

This stable pattern persists until early fall. But when the surface water cools to the same temperature as the depths, the lake begins to turn over and the fish scatter, resulting in some of the year's toughest fishing. You'll find some smallmouth feeding on shallow, rocky points; others, on deep rock bars. Worse yet, the locational patterns change quickly, depending mainly on the weather.

Late fall brings some stability, with smallmouth moving deeper to find slightly warmer water. You'll often find them in tight schools on steep-sloping structure, usually at depths of 25 to 40 feet, but sometimes even deeper. Feeding slows considerably when the water temperature dips into the low 40s, ending the season for most anglers.

Smallmouth Locations in Mesotrophic Lakes During ....

Early Spring
- Protected dark-bottomed bays.
- Boat canals and other protected channels off the main lake.

Spawning Period
- Protected sand-gravel bays.
- Protected sand-gravel shorelines in the main lake.

Sloping main-lake point.

Bulrushes.

- Shallow main-lake humps with a gravelly or rocky bottom.
- Gradually sloping main-lake points with a gravelly or rocky bottom.

- Hard-bottom areas with burushes or other emergent vegetation.

Post-Spawn
- Drop-off adjacent to gradually sloping spawning points.
- Breaklines adjacent to main-lake spawning flats.
- Breaklines off main-lake spawning humps.
- Shallow gravelly or rocky flats.

Summer and Early Fall
- Shallow gravelly or rocky flats near deep water.
- Rock piles or gravel bars on an otherwise soft bottom.
- Shallow to mid-depth main-lake humps with a gravelly or rocky bottom.
- Main-lake sand or gravel humps with submerged vegetation, particularly cabbage.
- Weedy saddles connecting two islands or a point and an island.
- Rocky, gravelly or sandy main-lake points with an extended lip that slopes moderately into deep water.
- Deep sandy or gravelly bays.
- Suspended over open water in cisco lakes.

Late Fall and Winter
- Deep, rocky humps.
- Irregular breaklines with a sharp drop into deep water.
- Sharp-sloping main-lake points.

Gravel hump surrounded by weeds.

OLIGOTROPHIC LAKES

Many oligotrophic lakes abound with smallmouth bass, yet anglers often have a hard time finding numbers of decent-sized fish. The problem is, with all the rocky structure, the entire lake looks like ideal smallmouth habitat, so it's hard to know where to start.

Many oli lakes are classified as "two-story" lakes, meaning that the depths are home to coldwater species, such as lake trout and whitefish, while warm- and coolwater species, like smallmouth bass, walleyes and northern pike, inhabit the shallower parts of the lake.

A glance at a lake map will give you a pretty good idea of where to look for smallmouth. If one part of the lake has a lot of 100-plus-foot water, that's where you'll find the lake trout. A section with a good deal of 20- to 30-foot water would be a much better bet for smallmouth. If you don't have a lake map, look for sections of the lake with clusters of islands rather than large expanses of open water. Smallmouth spend most of the year in these shallow-water zones but usually spend winter in deeper parts of the lake.

But not all oli lakes are deep and cold. Some have basins no deeper than 40 feet, meaning that the entire lake is smallmouth water.

Although the seasonal movement patterns of smallmouth in oli lakes are similar to those in meso lakes (p. 34), there are some significant differences.

In deep, cold oli lakes, for example, the water warms up so slowly in spring that smallmouth spawn at lower-than-normal temperatures. Instead of spawning at water temperatures in the low 60s, as they do in shallower lakes, they often spawn at temperatures in the mid 50s. And the spawning period is more compressed, sometimes lasting less than a week.

In meso lakes, which often have sandy basins, smallmouth are strongly drawn to rocky structure. But in oli lakes, where the basins tend to be rocky, smallmouth are drawn to sandy, weedy structure.

Many oli lakes and some deep meso lakes have large populations of ciscoes, which tend to suspend just below the thermocline in summer and may even come to the surface to feed on insects in the evening. Smallmouth follow the ciscoes, meaning that you may find them suspended or feeding on the surface in open water, far from any structure or cover.

Smallmouth Locations in Oligotrophic Lakes During...

Breaklines around island clusters.

Early Spring
- Protected dark-bottomed bays.
- Boat canals and other protected channels off the main lake.
- Gradually sloping breaklines near spawning areas.

Spawning Period
- Protected sandy or gravelly bays.
- Rocky or gravelly main-lake points.

Post-Spawn
- Points at the mouths of spawning bays.
- In deeper areas of mud-bottomed bays.
- Drop-offs adjacent to gradually sloping spawning points in main lake.
- Breaklines around island clusters.
- Shallow rocky reefs close to shore.

Summer and Early Fall
- Rocky, shallow to mid-depth humps with a gravelly or rocky bottom.
- Main-lake points with extended lips and bottoms of small boulders or broken rock rather than slab rock.
- Main-lake sand or gravel humps with submerged vegetation, particularly cabbage.
- Saddles connecting two islands or a point and an island.
- Breaklines around island clusters.
- Mouths of inlet streams.
- Suspended over open water in cisco lakes.

Mouth of inlet stream.

Late Fall and Winter
- Deep, main-lake reefs.
- Fast-sloping breaklines off main-lake flats.
- Sharp-sloping main-lake points.

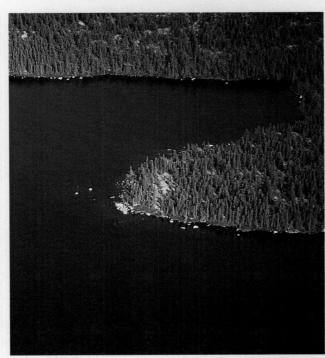

Point at the mouth of spawning bay.

EUTROPHIC LAKES

Finding smallmouths in most eutrophic lakes is easier than you may think. Because these lakes do not have a lot of good smallmouth habitat, the best spots should be pretty obvious.

If you can find a shallow, rocky point or shoreline flat, for example, that's probably where the fish will spawn. And a shallow, rocky hump in mid-lake will usually hold fish during the summer.

Many eutrophic lakes have surface temperatures in the 80s in midsummer, so anglers commonly assume they'll have to fish in deeper, cooler water. But that's almost always a mistake, because the deep waters lack sufficient oxygen to hold smallmouth during the summer months. In most cases, that means you won't find smallmouth deeper than 20 feet and, in highly eutrophic lakes, they may be no deeper than 10 feet.

Eutrophic lakes often have a shallow, bowl-shaped basin (p. 39), so smallmouth are drawn to subtle structural features. A gravel patch on an otherwise muddy bottom might be a key smallmouth spot, even if there is no depth change. And a 1- or 2-foot drop-off that would mean very little in a well-structured lake may hold a surprising number of smallmouth in a "dishpan" lake.

The fall turnover restores oxygen to all depths, so you may find smallmouth in the deepest part of a eutrophic lake in mid- to late fall. If you can find structure that breaks sharply into the depths, that's probably where you'll find the bass.

Very few ice fishermen target smallmouth in eutrophic lakes but, if you want to try, don't make the mistake of looking for them in their late-fall locations. Because of the high fertility, deepwater oxygen levels wane quickly after freeze-up, forcing the fish back into the shallows.

Smallmouth Locations in Eutrophic Lakes During...

Early Spring
- Along the first major drop-offs adjacent to spawning areas.
- Shallow mud-bottomed bays.
- Around mouths of creeks draining bog areas.

Spawning Period
- Protected sandy or gravelly bays.
- Gradually sloping main-lake points with a gravelly or rocky bottom.
- Natural rock or riprap areas along an otherwise sandy or muddy shoreline.

Post-Spawn through Early Fall and Mid-Winter
- Main-lake points with a gravelly or rocky bottom.
- Points and inside turns along the main breakline.
- Shallow rock piles or gravel bars in a main-lake basin.
- Patches of hard bottom in an area with a silty or mucky bottom.

Areas offering man-made riprap or rock.

Late Fall and Early Winter
- Fast-sloping areas along the main breakline.
- Main-lake points that drop sharply into deep water.
- Deep humps and rock piles.
- Deep holes in an otherwise shallow basin.

Gradually sloping gravel point.

Naturally rocky areas.

MAN-MADE LAKES

You can find smallmouth bass in every type of man-made lake, with the possible exception of shallow, "swampland" reservoirs.

Man-made lakes that fall into the "mid-depth" category are the best smallmouth producers. The category includes "hill-land" and "highland" reservoirs, which normally have moderate depths, medium to high clarity and moderate fertility. The creek arms are very distinct and may be several miles long.

Mid-depth reservoirs generally have plenty of rocky or gravelly spawning areas and an abundance of deep, hard-bottomed structure. Smallmouth foods, such as crayfish and shad, are plentiful. Some of the country's best trophy smallmouth waters, such as Dale Hollow Lake on the Kentucky-Tennessee border, and Pickwick Lake on the Alabama-Mississippi border, fall into this reservoir class.

Shallow reservoirs may also hold decent smallmouth populations, as long as they have fairly clear water and a basin that has not silted in to the point where little gravelly or rocky structure remains. Sometimes called "flatland" reservoirs, these impoundments are found on relatively level terrain. In the North, they're often referred to as "flowages."

Most shallow reservoirs have extensive stands of

flooded timber. The old river channel is much less distinct than in a deeper reservoir and may be silted in to the point where it is not noticeable. The creek arms, if any, are short and may look like nothing more than a bay.

On the other end of the spectrum are deep impoundments including "canyon" and "Canadian shield" reservoirs. The latter is just a natural Canadian shield lake that has been dammed to increase its volume, usually for power generation purposes. Smallmouth in these waters behave just as they do in natural shield lakes.

Canyon reservoirs are formed by damming a deep gorge, also for power generation. They're characterized by very long creek arms, some of which are so large that they're difficult to distinguish from the main body of the lake.

Because these lakes have so much deep, cold, infertile water, smallmouth grow slowly and seldom reach trophy size. In most deep reservoirs, a 5-pounder would be unusual.

The most important types of man-made smallmouth reservoirs are shown on the opposite page.

How Reservoir Types Differ

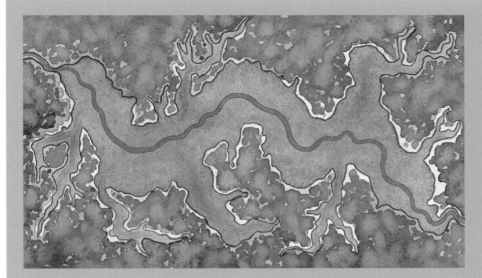

Highland/Hill-Land. These reservoirs have distinct creek arms, but the longest arms are considerably shorter than the main body of the lake. The old river channel and creek channels are well defined and may be as much as 50 feet deeper than the surrounding lake bed. Water clarity is moderate to high.

Flatland. The creek arms are much less distinct than in a highland or hill-land reservoir, and the old river channel and creek channels are not as well defined. In older reservoirs, the river and creek channels may not be apparent. Water clarity is moderate to low.

Canyon. The creek arms are very long and the longest ones may be almost as long as the main body of the reservoir. The old river channel may be difficult to recognize because the canyon walls slope sharply into the river gorge. Water clarity is very high.

HIGHLAND/ HILL-LAND RESERVOIRS

The diverse habitat in these classic smallmouth waters is a mixed blessing for anglers: It gives the fish everything they need to proliferate and grow to trophy size but, with so many locational options, finding them can be a challenge.

To locate smallmouth in winter, think deep. It's not unusual to find them at depths of 50 feet or more off steep main-lake points, along sharp-sloping cliff walls or in deep sections of the old river channel. Once smallmouth set up in these areas, they move very little until the water begins to warm in spring.

The first areas to warm are the creek arms, particularly shallow ones. As a rule, the shallowest creek arms are at the upper end of the reservoirs; the deepest ones, at the lower end. In some deep reservoirs, smallmouth in the upper creek arms spawn 3 to 4 weeks before those in the lower arms. A creek arm fed by an active stream will warm much earlier than a similar one with no inflow. The fish usually spawn at depths of 3 to 10 feet, but you may finds nests as deep as 15 feet in very clear lakes.

After spawning, most smallmouth move back to the main lake, although the deeper creek arms will hold fish all year. Typically, you'll find them at depths of 20 to 40 feet during the summer months, but they may move much shallower to feed in morning and evening.

Rocky main-lake points and mid-lake humps are prime summertime locations, although you may find smallmouth on any gradually sloping rocky or gravelly bank, especially if it abuts the old river channel. Here, the fish have easy access to deep, cool water.

Many highland and hill-land reservoirs have stands of flooded timber, but this type of cover is much less important to smallmouth than it is to largemouth. Nevertheless, you'll sometimes find smallmouth on a timbered flat along the old river channel or among trees or stumps near deep water.

As the water starts to cool in early fall, smallmouth begin to feed heavily. You'll often find them on the same structure they used in summer, but in much shallower water. When the water temperature falls below 50°F, however, the fish begin dropping into their deep wintering areas.

Many of these reservoirs undergo a fall drawdown to make room for spring runoff. The water level may plunge as much as 40 feet, forcing smallmouth in the shallow upper reaches of the lake into the lower reaches or deep main-lake holes or creek channels.

Smallmouth Locations in Highland/Hill-Land Reservoirs During...

Riprapped dam face.

Fencelines and other flooded cover.

Pre-Spawn through Spawn
- Back ends of shallow creek arms.
- Secondary and tertiary creek arms.
- Main-lake coves.
- Shallow, rocky points in main lake and creek arms.

Post-Spawn through Early Summer
- Shallow humps near shore.
- Shallow lips on rocky or gravelly points in main lake and creek arms.

- Eddies in tailwaters of upstream dam.

Mid-Summer through Mid-Fall
- Deep lips on rocky or gravelly points in main lake and creek arms.
- Points extending into old river channel.
- Timbered flats along old river channel and deep creek channels.
- Flooded roadbeds.
- Eddies in tailwaters of upstream dam.
- Fallen trees along steep banks.
- Main-lake humps near old river channel or other deep water.
- Around man-made fish attractors.
- Along riprapped roadbeds, bridges and dam facings.

Late Fall and Winter
- At base of deep main-lake points.
- Irregular breaklines with a sharp drop into deep water.
- Sharp-sloping main-lake points.
- Eddies in tailwaters of upstream dam.
- Along deep tree lines and fencerows.
- Deep portions of old river channel.

Timbered flats along old river channel.

Back end of a creek arm.

FLATLAND RESERVOIRS

Most flatland reservoirs were created by damming a river or stream in flat to gently rolling terrain, but some are preexisting lakes that were made a few feet deeper by construction of a low-head dam.

Although flatland reservoirs may be more than 100 feet deep at the lower end, the majority are only 30 to 60 feet deep. The deeper flatland reservoirs generally support the best smallmouth populations.

The habitat options for smallmouth in flatland reservoirs are much more limited than in highland or hill-land reservoirs. The fish are less likely to relate to the old river channel or creek channels, because these structures are relatively indistinct and may not even be noticeable. And because the creek arms are short or nonexistent, they may not draw smallmouth either.

But fewer habitat choices don't necessarily mean that smallmouth are easier to find. At spawning time, for example, you might find smallmouth nesting along any rocky or gravelly shoreline, meaning that you may have to scout miles of lakeshore to find the fish.

Because the clarity of most flatland reservoirs is fairly low, smallmouth spend most of their time in shallow water. Instead of nesting at depths of 3 to 10 feet, as they normally do in clear reservoirs, they're more likely to nest at 2 to 5 feet. And in summer, it's unusual to find smallmouth at depths greater than 20 feet.

The fish do seek out deep water in late fall, however. If the old river channel still exists, it will likely hold smallmouth through the winter. Otherwise, the fish will probably move to deep water at the lower end of the lake.

How To Catch Smallmouth Bass

Smallmouth Locations in Flatland Reservoirs During...

Pre-Spawn through Spawn
- Clean-bottomed areas in main-creek arms.
- Clean-bottomed areas in secondary creek arms.
- Main-lake coves.

Coves off the main lake.

- Rocky or gravelly main-lake points.
- Any gradually tapering rocky or gravelly shoreline.

Post-Spawn through Mid-Fall
- Shallow main-lake humps.
- Shallow lips on rocky or gravelly points in main lake and creek arms.
- Eddies in tailwaters of upstream dam.

- Rocky or gravelly shorelines of islands in the main lake.
- Timbered flats along old river channel (if distinct).
- Flooded roadbeds.
- Along flooded fencelines and tree rows.
- Around man-made fish attractors.
- Around bridge pilings.
- Along riprapped roadbeds, bridges and dam facings.

Late Fall and Winter
- At base of deep main-lake points.

Timber near old river channel.

- Along the dam facing.
- Along steep shorelines at lower end of lake.
- Around deep main-lake humps.
- Deepest part of old river channel.

Creek arm with woody cover.

Flooded trees.

CANYON RESERVOIRS

Found mainly in the western United States, canyon reservoirs have spectacular dams up to 700 feet high that impound water in the deep, narrow gorges between mountains.

Most canyon reservoirs were built for power generation and have relatively stable water levels, fluctuating no more than 20 feet over the course of the year. But some of these lakes were constructed for the main purpose of flood control; they're drawn down in fall to make room for spring runoff, so water levels may fluctuate as much as 100 feet. The latter type of lake obviously presents a greater challenge for anglers, because the fish are forced to move much more.

The fertility and clarity of a canyon reservoir may vary greatly from the upper end to the lower. Feeder streams at the shallow upper end commonly carry in nutrients from farm fields and cities, often resulting in dense algal blooms and low summertime oxygen levels. Although smallmouth sometimes frequent the upper reaches of these lakes in early spring and may even spawn there, they move downstream to deeper, clearer, cooler waters in summer.

Because the water is so clear, smallmouth go a lot deeper than you might expect. Even at spawning time, you'll find them in water as deep as 20 feet; in summer, they may descend to 80 feet.

Many deep, cold canyon reservoirs are better suited to salmonids, such as lake trout, rainbow trout and kokanee salmon, than they are to smallmouth bass and other warmwater gamefish. Although smallmouth abound in some canyon reservoirs, they tend to grow slowly because of the limited food supply. The high altitude of many of these lakes also contributes to the slow growth.

The majority of canyon reservoirs lack what most anglers would consider "typical smallmouth structure." The steep cliff walls do not provide the shelf area that the fish need for feeding and resting, but if you can find an unusual feature such as a "stair-step" break or a rock slide along an otherwise sheer wall, that's normally where you'll find the fish.

The lack of smallmouth structure also limits seasonal movements. Instead of seeking out entirely new structure as the season progresses, the fish usually stay on the structure they selected in early summer, gradually moving deeper as the winter approaches and the water cools.

In many canyon reservoirs, the creek arms are just as deep, wide and long as the main lake, and they provide similar habitat options. In this situation, you can expect smallmouth to carry out their entire life cycle in the main lake or a creek arm, with very little movement between the two.

Smallmouth Locations in Canyon Reservoirs During...

Pre-Spawn through Spawn
- Shallow coves in main lake and creek arms.
- Shallow gravel shoals, usually at a stream mouth.
- Gravel shoals in the stream itself.
- Shallow rock ledges covered with sand or gravel with scattered boulders for cover.

Stair-step cliff walls.

Post-Spawn through Mid-Fall
- Flats at the mouths of feeder creeks.
- Suspended just off of spawning shoals.
- Shallow rock or gravel bars.
- Coves in main lake and creek arms.

- Cliff walls with stair-step ledges.
- Rock ridges on shore that extend into the water.
- Rocky points with a shallow lip.
- Docks, brush clumps and other objects along sheer banks that offer shade.
- Rock slides along steep canyon walls.

Late Fall and Winter
- Same stair-step cliff walls used in summer but in deeper water.
- Same rock ridges used in summer but in deeper water.
- Same rocky points used in summer but in deeper water.
- Same rock slides used in summer but in deeper water.

Cliff walls offering ledges and broken rock.

Rock slides on canyon walls, especially back in coves and creek arms.

RIVERS & STREAMS

Smallmouth bass are much more current-oriented than largemouth, explaining why smallmouth thrive in every type of warmwater river or stream, with the exception of those that are badly polluted or stay muddy year-round.

Because smallmouth prefer a moderate current speed, they're seldom found in high-gradient streams that roar through steep valleys or in low-gradient streams that flow lazily through flat, agricultural areas.

Every smallmouth stream is unique and many defy classification. But, for the purposes of this book, we will discuss three major types: big rivers, small to mid-size streams, and creeks.

A big river, sometimes called a *mainstem* river, is the major waterway draining a large geographical area. It may vary in size from a block to more than a mile in width and usually has an extensive backwater system.

Small to medium-sized streams generally flow into mainstem rivers and are considerably smaller in size, usually less than 100 yards wide. They have no real backwater system, although they may be connected to sloughs, especially during periods of high water.

Most creeks flow into small or mid-sized streams. They

are no more than 30 feet wide and some are less than 10. Creeks rarely have any type of backwater area.

The best rivers and streams offer a diversity of habitat including firm-bottomed banks and shoals for spawning; areas of rocky bottom that produce crayfish and aquatic insects; shady, slackwater areas for resting; and deep holes for wintering. Creeks rarely offer this much diversity, but they can still hold smallmouth because the fish can migrate downstream to a larger stream to fulfill their needs.

Pages 50 to 55 explain how these stream types differ, how they relate to one another, and where to find the fish in each.

Mountain Smallmouths   *By Tom Carpenter*

Looking down on the magnificent New River Gorge, much of which is classified as a National River.

Readying an inflatable boat for an afternoon in the gorge.

One of the world's oldest rivers is called the New. It wanders, flows, tumbles and roars through awesome scenery and an incredible gorge in that motherlode of eastern mountains, West Virginia.

Yes, it is a river of contrasts. And it is full of smallmouth bass.

The Mountain Connection's Chris Ellis with a good New River smallmouth.

We fished it a couple lovely afternoons in spring, with the warm sun raking low over the top of the gorge. Turkeys in yonder hills beckoned Glenn Sapir, Bill Hollister and me for morning hunts, but afternoons were for bass.

The fishing is good and simple, and pure fun. You flow along with the river, a good guide at the oars keeping you where the fish are and pausing the custom inflatable boat in likely spots while you pitch jigs and tube baits to pockets behind boulders, slicks above riffles, eddies below riffles, seams between different currents ... anyplace where the flow breaks for a hungry smallmouth.

But the biggest fish—those 2- and 3-pounders (and many in the river will surpass 5 pounds)—often hold right in the faster water. These are active, aggressive, hungry fish with a strength and beauty as awesome as the surrounding mountains. It is some of the best

smallmouth fishing you will find anywhere.

And then, too soon, the drift would be over. Sun behind the wooded walls, the shadowed gorge was cold again. Having hauled in twenty or more bass, after turkey hunting from dawn to noon, we were the best kind of tired.

The Mountain Connection (Glade Springs Resort, 200 Lake Drive, Daniels, WV 25832; 1-800-634-5233; www.mountainconnection.com or www.gladesprings.com) outfits and guides smallmouth trips on the New, and offers a variety of other outdoor activities including rafting trips, turkey hunts, upland bird hunts and much more. Their equipment and services are top-notch. But more important, you will never find nicer people than those in "West Vahginny", to use the local and wonderful pronunciation.

A view of the New River gorge from atop a drift-boat fishing seat.

BIG RIVERS

The combination of diverse main channel habitat and lakelike backwaters explains why big rivers are top smallmouth bass producers.

Throughout most of the year, you won't find many smallmouth in the deepest part of the main channel, but the edges of the channel, called "the main channel border," often teem with smallmouth.

The main channel border includes a wide variety of man-made structure including wingdams; riprapped banks, roadways and dikes; bridge pilings and dock piers; and rock piles that hold channel markers and other navigational aids. Smallmouth use main channel habitat primarily in summer and fall, when the river is low and stable.

Backwater lakes, deep sloughs and marinas provide the stillwater habitat that smallmouth need for spawning. The fish also retreat to backwaters to escape the swift current during periods of high water.

The channels, or *cuts*, connecting the main channel with the backwaters also make excellent smallmouth habitat. These cuts often have not only wingdam-like structures called *closing dams* to restrict flow into the backwaters, but also lots of fallen trees and other woody cover that hold smallmouth. You'll find smallmouth in the cuts soon after they complete spawning, and some fish stay there well into the fall.

By late fall, most smallmouth have retreated to the deepest part of the main channel where they will spend the winter. If there is no deep water in a particular stretch of river, the fish will migrate to find a hole at least 30 feet deep. It's not unusual for the fish to move 30 miles or more to reach a prime wintering site.

Because big rivers eventually receive the flow of all the smaller streams and creeks, they are prone to major flooding. This means that a spot where you consistently caught smallmouth last year may not produce a single fish this year. For example, a severe flood may dump enough silt on a wingdam to cover the rocks and ruin its smallmouth drawing power. But the same flood may also deepen a shallow side channel or backwater and improve its smallmouth potential. Consequently, big-river anglers shouldn't be too set in their ways. After a major flood, it's a good idea to spend some time scouting for new smallmouth hangouts.

Smallmouth Locations in Big Rivers During...

Deep backwaters with woody cover.

Marinas with rock.

• Gravelly flats along main-channel border.
• Lips of rocky points.
• Eddies below major points.
• Around bridge piers and dock pilings.

Late Fall and Winter
• Deep holes in main channel, usually along outside bends.
• Any 30-foot-plus holes in backwaters.
•Deep washout holes in tailwaters of major dams.

Eddy below a point.

Early Spring
• Mud-bottomed sloughs and shallow backwaters that warm quickly in spring.
• Shallow back ends of deeper backwaters.
• Man-made boat channels and canals.
• Mouths of tributaries.

Spawning
• Backwaters with areas of rocky or gravelly bottom for nesting sites.

• Marinas with areas of rocky or gravelly bottom for nesting sites.
• Shallow gravel bars (in rivers that lack suitable backwater areas).
• Rocky shorelines sheltered from the current (in rivers that lack suitable backwater areas).

Post-Spawn through Mid-Fall
• Deep side channels, especially those with plenty of woody cover.
• Deep backwaters with weedy or woody cover.
• Wingdams with moderate current and exposed rock.
• Rock piles built to hold navigational aids.
• Riprapped shorelines and islands.

Wingdam.

Gravel bar.

Islands lined with rock.

SMALL TO MID-SIZE STREAMS

Fishing for smallmouth in smaller streams is a lot like fishing for trout. You're looking for stream reaches with clear water, moderate current and a meandering pool-riffle-run configuration. In fact, there are many streams that support trout in the cold upper reaches and smallmouth in the warmer lower reaches, with a transition area between the two zones that hold both.

In addition to the varied habitat, the best smallmouth streams also have deep holes that serve as wintering areas. Without these holes, the fish may have to migrate long distances to reach deeper water in a larger river.

As the water begins to warm in spring, smallmouth move out of the wintering holes and begin their migration, usually upstream, to their spawning areas. They nest along banks with light current and a rock, gravel or sand bottom. As in most other waters, the prime nesting sites have a boulder or log on one side to protect the nest from predators. Rarely do the fish nest in more than 3 feet of water. If the stream does not have good spawning habitat, smallmouth may swim up small tributaries to find suitable conditions.

Once spawning has been completed, the fish remain in shallow water, usually stationing themselves along a current break where they can rest in slack water and dart out to grab drifting food. But as the summer wears on, they look for deeper pools, preferably those that have a shallow riffle area just upstream. This way, they can rest in the deep water and make short feeding forays into the riffle area to find crayfish and lar-val insects. The best smallmouth pools have a rocky or gravelly bottom with plenty of cover such as boulders, fallen trees, rocky ledges or undercut banks.

Cooling water in fall activates the smallmouth again, causing them to feed for longer periods. Some fish, usually the biggest ones, may remain in the deep pools; but the majority move to the same current breaks they used after spawning. The fish continue to feed heavily until the water temperature reaches the low 50s.

By the time the water has dropped to the mid 40s, most smallmouth have left the shallows and retreated to their deep wintering holes. They feed only sporadically through the winter, although anglers who know the location of the wintering holes catch fish using slow, live-bait presentations.

Smallmouth Locations in Small to Mid-Size Rivers During...

Early Spring through Spawning
- Seasonally flooded pools, sloughs or oxbows.
- In slow or slackwater zone at the tail of an island.
- Eddies below points.
- Rocky, gravelly or sandy banks sheltered from the current.
- Sand or gravel bars on inside bends.

Eddy below a rocky point.

Sandbar.

- Midstream sand or gravel bars in low-water years.
- Tributary streams that offer good spawning habitat.

Post-Spawn
- Eddies below large boulders.
- Eddies formed by logjams, fallen trees and brush piles.
- Eddies below low-head dams.
- Eddies below points.
- Along any noticeable current seam.

Early Summer through Early Fall
- Deep pools with a rocky or gravelly bottom.
- Riffles just upstream from deep pools.
- Beneath deep undercut banks. on outside bends.
- Deep eddies below points.
- Eddies below low-head dams.
- Steep, jagged, rocky ledges.
- Deep eddies below logjams and fallen trees.
- Eddies below bridge pilings.
- Around spring areas that cool the water.

Mid-Fall
- Eddies below large boulders.
- Eddies formed by logjams, fallen trees and brush piles.
- Eddies below low-head dams.
- Eddies below points.
- Along any noticeable current seam.

Eddy below large boulder.

Late Fall and Winter:
- Deep holes along outside bends.
- Deep holes below dams.
- Deep holes in connecting river.

Rocky bank out of the main current.

CREEKS

Many anglers, as kids, developed a lifetime love affair with smallmouth bass by fishing on a small creek near their home. The fish didn't run very big, but they were plentiful and willing to bite.

Creeks are the most overlooked type of smallmouth water. Although the habitat options in most creeks are limited, the fish do surprisingly well if they can find adequate depth, cover and food.

In the majority of creeks, food is not a problem; there's a good supply of creek minnows including shiners, chubs and dace. Depth and cover are usually the limiting factors. As a rule, a good smallmouth creek should have pools at least 6 feet deep with plenty of boulders, logs and undercut banks to provide hiding spots.

Some creeks have an abundance of man-made structure and cover that improves their smallmouth potential. A road culvert, for example, often has a washout hole on the downstream side that holds dozens of smallmouth. The fish sometimes line up to feed along the current break created by the culvert's flow. Other common types of man-made cover include bridge pilings and huge boulders placed along the bank to prevent erosion of adjacent roads. These boulders make especially good cover because the fish can hide in the crevices to escape the swift current during a flood.

Because of their limited habitat, creek smallmouth move a lot less than their relatives in larger rivers and streams. In northern creeks, however, smallmouth usually abandon the creek in winter, migrating downstream to find a deep wintering hole in a larger stream. Such migrations may not be necessary in southern streams because the winter conditions are much less severe.

Smallmouth Locations in Creeks During...

Eddy below fallen tree.

Early Spring through Spawning
- Seasonally flooded pools and sloughs.
- Eddies below sharp bends.
- Rocky, gravelly or sandy banks sheltered from the current.
- Sand or gravel bars.

Post-Spawn through Mid Fall
- Deep pools.
- Riffles just upstream from deep pools.
- Eddies below boulders.
- Beneath deep undercut banks.
- Eddies formed by logjams, fallen trees and brush piles.
- Eddies below culverts.
- Crevices between bank-protecting boulders.
- Eddies below sharp bends.
- Along any noticeable current seam.

Current seam.

Late Fall and Winter:
- Deep holes along outside bends (southern creeks).
- Deep holes in connecting river.

Rocky bank sheltered from the current.

Eddy below boulder or man-made obstructions.

THE GEAR

*Y*ou don't need a lot of fancy equipment to catch smallmouth —just the right equipment.

Medium-power spinning outfit.

RODS & REELS

When you hook a small-mouth and it makes a spectacular leap before heading for the depths with a line-sizzling run, you'll be glad you spent a few extra bucks to buy a reel with a smooth drag. But as hard as smallmouth fight, their bites may be surprisingly light. So it pays to invest in a sensitive, high-modulus graphite rod.

Many smallmouth anglers make the mistake of using an outfit that's much too light, thinking that it will add to the enjoyment of catching these scrappy fighters. While that may be the case, a light outfit can cause problems—for you and the fish. Here's why:

• With light gear, you can't keep the fish away from heavy cover. If it makes a run into a log jam or weed patch, you're out of luck.

• Light gear is fine for tossing spinners, jigs, split-shot rigs and other light lures, but you'll need a heavier outfit to cast good-sized plugs, spinnerbaits, Carolina rigs, etc.

• With a light outfit, you'll have to fight these never-say-die battlers to near exhaustion, reducing the chances of a successful live release.

Some serious smallmouth anglers carry 6 to 8 outfits for specific fishing purposes but, for the majority of fishermen, the outfits described below will handle just about any presentation. We'll also take a look at fly-fishing gear.

Spinning Outfit

A 6- to 6½-foot, medium-power spinning rod can be used for most light-lure and live-bait presentations. A rod with a fast tip works best for jig fishing, but a slow tip is a better choice for live-bait presentations because the fish won't feel as much resistance when it picks up the bait.

Pair this rod with a quality wide-spool, front-drag spinning reel.With a wide spool, your line will flow off the reel more easily, improving casting performance. And a front drag has a much larger friction surface than a rear drag, so it's smoother and less likely to stick.

Baitcasting Outfit

When fishing with crankbaits or most topwaters, select a medium-power baitcasting rod from 5½ to 6½ feet long. It should have a fairly soft tip that allows a fish to take the lure deeper than it otherwise would. A softer tip also flexes more on the hookset so you won't pull the lure away from the fish too quickly.

For bladebaits, tailspinners and other jigging lures weighing ⅜ ounce or more, you'll need a 6- to 6½-foot, medium-heavy to heavy-power baitcasting rod with a fast tip and an extra-long handle. This rod also works well for casting spinnerbaits.

A wide-spool baitcasting reel with a gear ratio of at least 6:1 is a good choice for either of these rods because it gives you good casting distance along with a fast retrieve.

Baitcasting outfit.

Flippin' Outfit

Flipping jigs or other lures into tight spots is easiest with a "flippin' stick," which is a heavy-power, fast-action rod about 7½ feet in length. The rod telescopes down to about 6½ feet so it will fit into a rod locker.

Because you'll need heavy line for flippin' (p. 145), you'll want a sturdy baitcasting reel, preferably one with a thumb-bar spool release. With the short casts, there is no need for a wide spool or a high gear ratio.

Flippin' sticks come in handy for many other kinds of smallmouth fishing as well. They're a good choice for deep jigging, buzzbaiting and any presentation that requires long-distance casting.

Flippin' outfit.

Fly-fishing outfit.

Fly-Fishing Outfit

To cast big, wind-resistant flies and to handle the powerful runs of a good-sized smallmouth, you'll need a fairly beefy fly rod. A 6-weight will normally do the job, but most anglers prefer a 7- or 8-weight about 8½ feet long. Shorter rods (7½ feet or less) are popular among small-stream fishermen because they make it easier to cast in a narrow stream corridor with trees or high weeds on both sides.

Although most manufacturers do not designate the action of their fly rods, it's a good idea to select a rod that bends mainly at the tip (fast action) rather than gradually over the entire length (slow action). A fast-action rod makes it much easier to handle large "bass bugs" and poppers, which are considerably heavier than most other kinds of flies.

You don't need to spend a fortune on a fly reel for smallmouth fishing. Most any "single-action" reel with adequate line capacity will do the job. With a single-action reel, you have a 1:1 retrieve ratio, meaning that the spool turns once for each turn of the handle. That's adequate for most smallmouth fishing situations.

But if you think you'll have to take up line more quickly, choose a multiplying reel. "Multipliers" give you a retrieve ratio of 1.5:1 to 3:1, but they have more moving parts than a single action so they're a little heavier.

A good-sized smallmouth can sizzle off 50 yards of fly line in a heartbeat, so it pays to have a reel with an adjustable drag. The most common type is a "ratchet-and-pawl" drag, which has an adjustable spring to keep the pawl pushed against the ratchet, putting pressure on the spool and making a clicking sound.

LINES & KNOTS

Although monofilament is the overwhelming choice of most experienced smallmouth anglers, you may need other kinds of lines for specific purposes. Here's a rundown on the most important kinds of lines used in smallmouth fishing, along with the best knots:

Monofilament

There are several good reasons why mono is so popular among smallmouth fishermen:

• Smallmouth usually live in clear water, so they can easily see braided line or even heavy mono.

• The stretch factor of mono is a plus for most lure

and live-bait presentations. A smallmouth generally flares its gills and sucks in a volume of water to inhale your bait; if your line doesn't stretch, it may prevent the fish from taking the bait deep enough.

• A little stretch also reduces the chances of a break-off. When a smallmouth makes one of its patented power runs, the extra stretch of mono gives you a "cushion."

• Because mono absorbs water much more slowly than braided lines, it works better for topwater fishing. If you tie superline to a surface lure, the line sinks almost immediately, pulling the nose of the

lure under when you retrieve. With mono, the nose stays up as it should, so the lure has better action.

Light line is the rule in most smallmouth angling. If you're fishing in an area with little weedy or woody cover, you can probably get by with 6-pound mono and would rarely need anything stronger than 8-pound. Light-tackle specialists commonly use 4-pound. When flippin' in downed trees or brush piles, however, you'll need 17- to 20-pound test to minimize the number of break-offs and horse a fish out of the cover before it can tangle you around a limb.

Always select a premium grade of mono and use a color that blends in with the water you're fishing. In very clear water, for instance, clear mono is the best choice. In water with a greenish tint, use green mono.

Limp mono works best for the majority of smallmouth-fishing situations. But if you'll be working an area with lots of rocks or other objects that could scuff your line, use hard-finish, abrasion-resistant mono.

Tough-finish line (left) is resistant to fraying in rocks or snags, but limp line (right) works better.

Superline

For deep trolling and jigging, superline is a much better choice than mono. Here's why:

• The thin diameter of superline allows it to cut through the water with much less resistance, meaning that you can troll considerably deeper without adding more weight.

• When you're jigging in deep water, the low stretch of superline enables you to feel strikes more easily and get a stronger hookset than you could with mono. But you may want to splice on a 6- to 12-foot mono leader using a double uni-knot (p. 65) to decrease visibility and provide a little cushion.

Because superline has virtually no stretch, it's not a good idea to use a stiff rod. If you do, you'll risk breaking the line or rod on the hookset and possibly tearing the hooks out of the fish.

Fly Line

When fishing smallmouth with the heavy, wind-resistant bugs so popular among fly anglers, you'll need a floating line with either a weight-forward or bass-bug taper. The latter is just a weight-forward line, but with a shorter, denser head intended to punch bulky flies into the wind.

You can use the same line for fishing streamers, nymphs, crayfish imitations or leech patterns, but if you want to get these subsurface flies down in water more than 5 feet deep, you'll probably need a sink-tip line.

The weight of your line (usually 6 to 8) should match the weight of your rod, although you can easily cast a line one size smaller or larger than the rod weight. In other words, a 7-weight rod could handle a 6-, 7- or 8-weight line. Before spooling on the fly line, be sure to fill your reel with at least 100 yards of 20- to 30-pound-test Dacron backing.

You'll need a heavy leader for turning over big, bulky flies. A good all-around choice is a leader about 9 feet long with a 40-pound-test butt tapering to an 8-pound-test tippet.

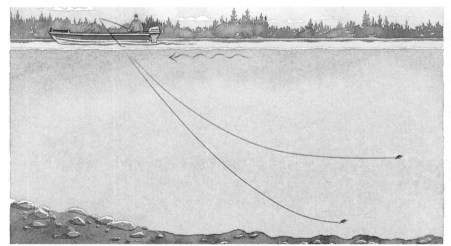

Because of its thin diameter, superline (blue) gets a trolled crankbait 50 to 75 percent deeper than monofilament of the same strength (red).

Fly lines have a 3-part code to designate taper, weight and flotation. This box contains a weight-forward (WF) taper, 4-weight, floating (F) fly line.

Important Bass-Fishing Knots

Attaching Line to Spool—Mono or Superline: Arbor Knot

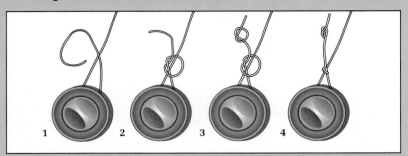

The arbor knot is so named because it tightens firmly around the arbor, preventing the line from slipping when you reel.

(1) Pass the line around the spool; *(2)* wrap the free end around the standing line and make an overhand knot; *(3)* make an overhand knot in the free end; *(4)* snug up the knot by pulling on the standing line; the knot should tighten firmly around the arbor.

Attaching Hook or Lure—Mono or Superline: Trilene Knot

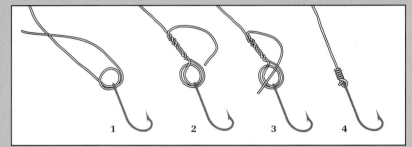

The Trilene knot has a double loop around the hook eye and is one of the strongest hook-attachment knots.

(1) Form a double loop by passing the free end through the hook eye twice; *(2)* wrap the free end around the standing line 4-5 times; *(3)* pass the free end through the double loop; *(4)* pull on the standing line and hook to snug up the knot.

Attaching Hook or Lure—Mono or Superline: Palomar Knot

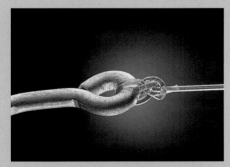

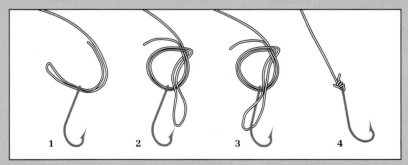

The palomar knot, like the Trilene knot, has a double loop around the hook eye. But some anglers find it easier to tie.

(1) Form a double line, then push it through the hook eye; *(2)* with the double line, make an overhand knot around the standing line and free end; *(3)* put the hook through the loop; *(4)* hold the hook while pulling on the standing line and free end to snug up the knot.

How To Catch Smallmouth Bass

Attaching Lure to Line—Mono: Loop Knot

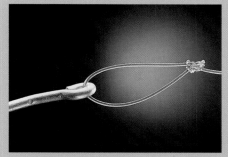

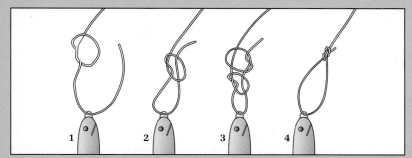

A loop knot allows your lure to swing more freely, so it has better action than a lure that is snubbed down tightly.

(1) Make an overhand knot near the end of the line and put the free end through the lure eye; *(2)* pass the free end through the overhand knot; *(3)* with the free end, make an overhand knot around the standing line (where you tie the second overhand determines the size of the loop); *(4)* tighten the overhand knots and pull the standing line to snug up the knot.

Splicing Lines of Similar Diameter—Mono: Blood Knot

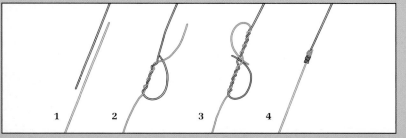

A blood knot looks complex, but is quite simple to tie. Don't try it with lines of greatly different diameters or different materials.

(1) Hold the lines alongside each other, with the ends facing opposite directions; *(2)* wrap one line around the other 4-5 times, and pass the free end between the two lines, as shown; *(3)* repeat step 2 with the other line; *(4)* pull on both lines to snug up the knot.

Splicing Mono of Different Diameter or Mono to Superline: Double Uni-Knot

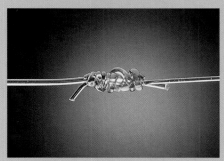

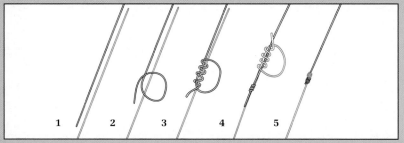

The double uni-knot is the best way to splice mono to superline. It works well for any lines of different material or diameter.

(1) Hold the lines alongside each other, with the ends facing opposite directions; *(2)* form a loop with one of the lines, as shown; *(3)* pass the free end through the loop and around the standing line 4-5 times and then snug up the knot; *(4)* repeat steps 2 and 3 with the other line; *(5)* pull on both lines to draw the two knots together.

A bass boat gets you there in a hurry—and you'll fish in comfort.

How To Catch Smallmouth Bass

BOATS & MOTORS

A well-equipped bass boat is the ultimate tool in large-mouth fishing and is no less valuable when you're pursuing smallmouth, especially on big reservoirs where you may have to run 20 miles or more to reach a prime fishing spot. Not only will a bass boat get you to your spot in a hurry, its wide, shallow hull minimizes the effects of the wind and gives you a very stable fishing platform.

But there is no single boat that suits all smallmouth-fishing situations. A bass boat is unnecessary on smaller smallmouth waters and would be impossible to use on most streams and many remote northern lakes. In these spots, a canoe or small jon boat is a much better choice.

Here's what to look for when selecting a boat for smallmouth fishing:

Bass Boat

A 16- to 18-foot fiberglass bass boat powered by a 50- to 125-hp outboard is a good choice for the majority of smallmouth waters. But if you'll be plying big rivers or reservoirs, you may want to consider a fiberglass bass boat up to 20 feet in length with a 150- to 225-hp outboard. These boats attain speeds of 50 to 70 mph.

Aluminum bass boats are also popular among small-mouth anglers. They're much less expensive and will do just about everything a fiberglass model will do, but they give you a rougher ride. You can buy aluminum bass boats ranging from 16 feet long with a 30-hp outboard to 19 feet long with a 150-hp outboard.

A well-equipped bass boat has the following features:

• Elevated casting decks in the bow and stern, equipped with swivel chairs or butt seats.

• An insulated, aerated live well with an aeration timer to conserve battery power.

• A rod locker at least 7 feet long to accommodate flippin' sticks and other long bass rods.

• Velcro deck straps to secure fishing rods on high-speed runs.

• Battery compartments large enough for at least 3 large marine batteries.

• Dry-storage compartments for lure boxes, clothing, life jackets and other items that will mildew or rust if they get wet.

• A manual bilge pump and possibly an automatic bilge pump that turns on whenever the bilge water reaches a certain level.

• An onboard battery charger that will charge all of your boat batteries at once.

• An outboard with power trim to maximize high-speed performance, and power tilt for motoring in very shallow water.

Big-Water V-Hull

Because of its shallow hull, a bass boat is not a good choice on large, wind-swept lakes. Many natural lakes in the North, for example, have round basins 10 or more miles wide, so waves more than 5 feet high are not uncommon.

In this situation, a 16- to 19-foot boat with a deep-V hull is

The flared hull of a fiberglass V-hull kicks water to the side, keeping you dry and giving you a smooth ride.

much safer. The V-shaped bow parts the waves, yet the bottom is flat enough to give you good stability. These boats, commonly used for walleye, muskie and pike fishing, are usually powered by 50- to 150-hp outboards.

Deep-Vs come in aluminum and fiberglass models. Although the fiberglass boats are heavier and generally more expensive, their hulls can be molded into the ideal flare for throwing water to the side and offering a smoother ride.

Many anglers prefer tiller-operated semi-Vs, especially for backtrolling (below). Outfitted with a powerful transom-mount trolling motor, this type of boat offers the ultimate in boat control.

A well-equipped deep-V has most of the same features as a bass boat, but you may want to install splash guards for backtrolling. And if you prefer a tiller model boat, look for one with a good-sized electronics box to protect your depth finders and other electronics from spray.

The flat bottom of a jon boat makes it an exceptionally stable craft.

Jon Boat

The overwhelming choice among stream fishermen, a jon boat is the ideal craft for navigating very shallow water. A "tunnel jon" (below) or a regular jon boat with a jet-drive outboard can easily skim over riffles or flats only a few inches deep. A jon boat's flat-bottom design provides excellent stability, so the craft is not nearly as "tippy" as a canoe or small semi-V.

A jon boat with a semi-V bow cuts through the waves more easily than one with a square bow.

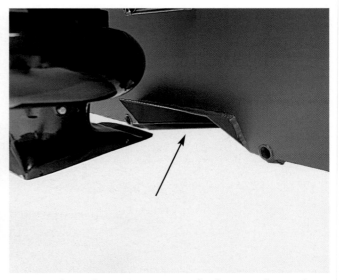

A tunnel jon has a cutout on the bottom (arrow) that funnels water to the propeller while protecting the hull from rocks.

How To Catch Smallmouth Bass

Another reason jon boats are so popular among stream fishermen: They are very light for their size, so a pair of anglers can easily carry a 14- to 16-footer down to the water on streams that do not have a developed boat access site.

Most jon boats have the standard square-bow design but, for bigger rivers or lakes, a model with a semi-V bow is a better choice. The V-shaped bow helps part the waves, yet the boat still has the flat bottom necessary for a shallow draft and good stability.

A 6- to 10-hp outboard provides all the power you need for a 14-foot jon boat, but most anglers prefer a 15- to 25-hp motor on a 16-footer. Jet-drive outboards are much less efficient than propeller-driven models, so you'll need about 30 percent more horsepower to attain the same speed.

Canoe

A canoe is the only craft practical for fishing very small streams and for portaging into remote lakes. And if you're fishing a river that has impassible rapids, all you have to do is pick up your canoe and carry it around to the other side of the dangerous water.

Aluminum canoes are widely used because they're durable, fairly light and relatively inexpensive. But canoes made of synthetic materials like Kevlar and ABS are rapidly gaining in popularity and, even though they're more expensive and less durable, their extremely light weight makes them ideal for portaging.

In order to use an outboard, you'll need a square-stern canoe or one with a side-mount bracket. Although some large canoes will take a motor up

A side-mount bracket enables you to attach an electric trolling motor or small outboard to a standard canoe.

to 10 hp, most anglers use 2- to 4-hp motors to conserve weight. And if you don't have far to go, you may be able to get by with an electric trolling motor. It will move a canoe at surprising speed.

You'll need a lightweight canoe for portaging into remote waters.

ELECTRONICS

If you like to catch small-mouth by wading a small stream, you don't have to concern yourself with electronics. But good electronics are a must in practically every other smallmouth-fishing situation. Here are some guidelines for selecting the best electronics for smallmouth fishing:

Depth Finder

Anglers who drift small streams in canoes or jon boats rely on a flasher to help them find deep holes. But in most lakes and bigger rivers, you'll want a quality liquid-crystal or video graph that will not only help you pinpoint likely structure, but also help you spot fish.

A good graph should have the following features:

• A high-resolution screen that gives you enough detail so that you can distinguish fish from schools of baitfish or clumps of insects. As a rule, a liquid-crystal should have a minimum of 200 vertical pixels. Resolution is not really an issue in selecting a video; they employ a CRT screen much like that of a TV set, so they have excellent resolution.

• A fast sweep speed that enables you to graph fish while moving at speeds of up to 10 mph. If your unit has a slow sweep speed, it will not "keep up" if you attempt to sound at high speed.

• A "zoom" feature that enables you to focus on a particular part of the water column and blow it up on the screen for better visibility.

Besides these basic features, some top-quality graphs also have dual trans-

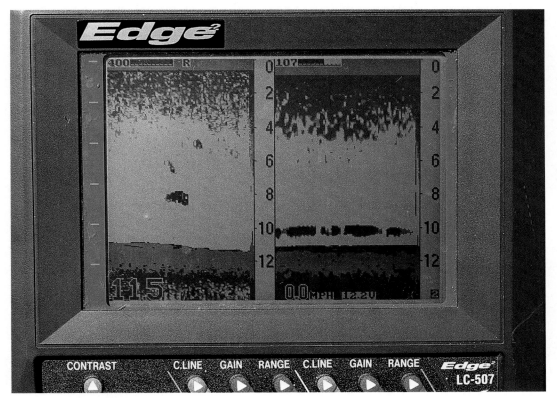

A split-screen feature allows you to view a large area of the bottom with a wide-angle transducer (left half of screen) yet spot bottom-hugging fish with the narrow-angle transducer (right half of screen).

ducers. The wide-angle transducer (cone angle up to 45°) allows you to view a large area of the bottom while the narrow angle (cone angle as little as 8°) helps you see bottom-hugging fish that the wide-angle transducer may miss. Some graphs have a split-screen feature that displays readouts from both transducers at once.

Other handy graph features include a wide screen to provide more "history," a contrast adjustment that helps you better see the screen in differing light conditions, a surface-temperature readout and a speed indicator.

Depth-Finder Tips

For high-speed sounding, mount your transducer so the leading edge is slightly below the boat bottom, and the transducer's bottom is tipped down at a 5- to 10-degree angle.

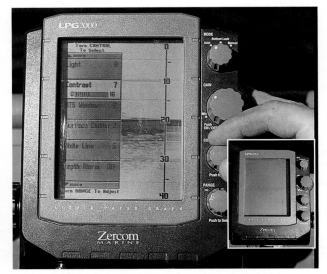

A graph with a contrast adjustment gives you an easily readable display under any light conditions. Otherwise, bright sun may "wash out" the display to the point that it's barely readable (inset).

A permanent mount GPS unit has a large, easy-to-read screen.

GPS

If you do much small-mouth fishing on large bodies of water, a GPS unit will save you a lot of time. Not only will it help you find your fishing spots in a hurry, it makes it easier to get back to the landing—even at night or in foggy weather.

A GPS unit is especially valuable if you're fishing an unfamiliar lake that has a map showing GPS coordinates. Then you can punch these coordinates into your GPS unit and go right to a particular spot.

In selecting a GPS, your major decision is whether to buy a permanent-mount or handheld unit. There are pluses and minuses to both:

A permanent-mount has a larger screen that is much easier to read, especially in plotter mode. It also has more keys, so you do not have to punch a complicated key sequence to reach the desired data screen. To enter a way-point, for instance, you simply push the waypoint button and the waypoint screen appears. And because a permanent-mount operates off your boat's electrical system, you don't have to worry about running out of battery power.

Handheld units are surprisingly inexpensive and have the obvious advantages of being small and portable. You can take a handheld with you when fishing in a friend's boat or even use it for hunting and other outdoor activities.

Handheld GPS.

Underwater Video Camera

Every angler has faced this dilemma: You're seeing lots of fish on your graph, but they won't bite. You're hoping it's a school of smallmouth, but you have an inkling that they could be carp, suckers or some other kind of roughfish.

To find out for sure, drop down an underwater video camera and have a look. Only then will you know whether it's worth sticking around or heading for a new spot.

An underwater video camera has another useful smallmouth-fishing application. It allows you to explore structure, such as a sunken island, to find a rocky section that holds crayfish and will, at some point, draw smallmouth.

Underwater video takes the guesswork out of fish scouting.

Surface Temperature Gauge

You can catch smallmouth over a wide water-temperature range, so you can certainly get by without a temperature gauge. But there are times when it helps to know the water temperature.

A temperature gauge is especially useful in spring, when the water temperature is below the 50°F mark. Smallmouth in water this cold are usually lethargic and difficult to catch. But certain parts of a lake may warm up more quickly than others, drawing baitfish and activating the smallmouth bite. With a surface temperature gauge, you can easily pinpoint these areas and get in on some fast action.

Some electric trolling motors have a built-in surface temperature gauge.

WADING GEAR

For many anglers, the most enjoyable type of smallmouth fishing is wading in a small stream. You don't need an expensive boat outfitted with the latest in electronic gadgetry—it's just you against the fish.

But unless you like to fish in shorts and tennis shoes, you do need a good pair of waders or hip boots. Here are the main considerations in making your selection:

Style

Waders and hip boots both come in boot-foot and stocking-foot models. Boot-foot wading gear fits more loosely so you can slip it on or off easily. But if you're wading in a stream with a soft bottom, the boots may stick in the mud and pull off when you walk.

Stocking-foot wading gear has separate boots that give you excellent ankle support. It won't pull off when you walk in the mud, and is usually lighter than boot-foot gear.

Material

You can buy a pair of rubber waders at your local discount store for the price of a dinner for two. But rubber waders are heavy and too hot for most summertime fishing. Here are some better choices:

Gore-Tex. The most comfortable wading gear is made from Gore-Tex or other breathable fabrics. These materials keep you dry yet allow enough air to pass through to keep you cool.

Neoprene. An excellent choice in cool weather, neoprene has good insulating qualities and is more flexible than other kinds of wading gear. And should you trip and fall, it will keep you afloat.

Nylon. Used mainly in warm weather, nylon wading gear has no insulation and is very light. It's also less expensive than Gore-Tex or neoprene.

Nylon waders are perfect for warm-weather smallmouth work.

Here's a tip to keep your waders in good shape: After a day of fishing, use a hair dryer to get rid of any moisture inside your wading gear.

Type of Sole

When selecting wading gear, most anglers give little thought to the type of sole. But it pays to have the right sole, especially if you'll be wading on slippery rocks.

Most inexpensive wading gear has rubber soles with ridges or cleats molded in. These soles are fine if you'll be fishing on a sandy or muddy bottom, but they have poor traction on rocks.

Felt soles have much better traction, and work well on most any kind of bottom, including moss-covered rocks. For wading in fast current where good traction is a must, use felt soles with metal studs. The studs also increase the life of felt soles.

If the stream is small, hip boots might do the job for you.

Tips for Using Wading Gear

With stocking-foot wading gear, wear ankle guards to keep gravel out of your boots.

Carry a tube of adhesive sealant in case your wading gear springs a leak.

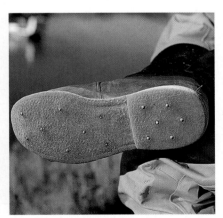

For the very best traction, use felt soles with metal studs.

Equip your fishing vest with everything you need for a day on the stream.

ACCESSORIES

You don't need all the items mentioned here to catch smallmouth, but some will surely help you land a few more fish or, at the very least, make your fishing experience more enjoyable.

Here are some of the accessories commonly used by avid smallmouth anglers:

• **Fishing Vest.** If you like to catch smallmouth by wading in a small stream or along a lakeshore, you'll probably want to invest in a fishing vest similar to those used by trout fishermen.

A fishing vest should be large enough that you can wear a jacket underneath it in cool weather. It should have lots of pockets with zippers or Velcro fasteners to prevent loss of equipment, and a loop at the back of the collar for attaching a landing net.

If you'll be wading in deep water, select a "shorty" vest that will keep your gear dry.

• **Hook Remover.** Most smallmouth anglers release the majority of the fish they catch, so it's important to carry a needlenose pliers, hemostat or "Hookout" to minimize injury to the fish. Digging the hook out with your fingers or a big pair of pliers may damage the gills or rip the fish's throat.

• **Marker Buoys.** If you're fishing a sunken island, an

A Hookout is ideal for removing a deeply embedded hook because the tiny jaws make the tool easy to maneuver in a tight space.

You can buy commercially made "stealth markers" (shown) but some anglers make their own using a film canister, string and sinker.

A good hook file will restore a damaged hook point in a hurry.

extended lip of a point or other structure that's difficult to pinpoint visually, you'll need one or more marker buoys.

Of course, the downside to tossing out a marker is that you'll attract unwelcome company. To minimize that problem, use a small, black-colored "stealth" marker.

• **Compartmentalized Tackle System.** Most versatile smallmouth anglers have a tackle-storage system that consists of plastic lure boxes for each type of artificial they use, as well as boxes for live-bait rigging. All these boxes fit into a larger tackle pack; this way, you don't have to dig through a big, messy tackle box to find the equipment you need.

• **Hook Sharpener.** A hook file or hone is one accessory that should not be considered optional. The hooks on many quality lures are surprisingly dull and even if you substitute chemically sharpened hooks, they may lose their needle-sharp points by bumping on rocks. A good file or hone will quickly take care of the problem.

• **Measuring Device.** Many smallmouth waters now have size limits so if you plan on keeping any fish, you'll need a tape measure or, better yet, a measuring board to get an accurate length measurement.

• **Polarized Sunglasses.** Smallmouth spend a lot of their time in shallow water where you can see them—if you're wearing polarized sunglasses. The glasses also help protect your eyes from harmful ultraviolet rays.

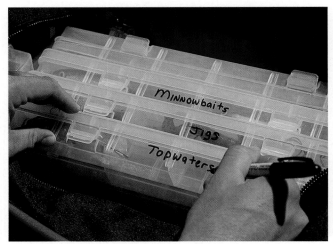

Use a waterproof marker to label each box in your tackle system.

Polarized sunglasses are a must if you'll be sight fishing. Make sure the glasses you buy have UV protection.

LURES, BAITS & HOW TO USE THEM

*F*or consistent smallmouth-fishing success, you have to know when, where and how to use each important lure or bait.

SMALLMOUTH-FISHING BASICS

Anglers who spend most of their time fishing for largemouth bass often have a hard time catching smallmouth because they rely on the same locational patterns, the same lures and the same presentations. But you can greatly improve your smallmouth-fishing results by remembering one important principle: Smallmouth are not largemouth. Refer to page 9 for a summary of the biological differences that can impact your fishing.

To become a successful smallmouth angler, you must learn to tailor your fishing technique to the situation at hand. But regardless of what method you use, there are certain smallmouth-fishing principles that always apply.

• **Smallmouth prefer smaller baits than largemouth.** That's not to say a good-sized smallmouth won't hit a big tandem spinnerbait or 8-inch shiner. But day in and day out, you'll have better success using smaller lures and baits. While a largemouth fisherman might select an 8-inch plastic worm, for example, a savvy smallmouth angler would pick a 4-incher.

• **Smallmouth prefer drab colors.** While largemouth are often drawn to lures with bright or gaudy colors, smallmouth generally favor the natural look. This explains why a smoke- or crawfish-colored grub, for instance, will usually outproduce a red-and-white or chartreuse grub. In very murky water, however, the reverse may hold true.

• **Fish a little deeper for smallmouth than you would for largemouth.** This is a solid rule most of the time,

Smallmouth prefer the natural look.

although there will be instances where both smallmouth and largemouth are found in only a foot or two of water. Where smallmouth share the same water with walleyes, smallmouth will usually be a little shallower.

Because of their smaller mouth, smallmouth favor smaller baits than largemouth.

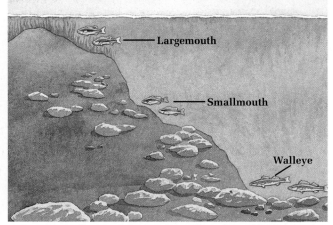

Where smallmouth, largemouth and walleye share the same structure, walleye will generally be deepest; largemouth, shallowest.

Smallmouth are object-oriented, commonly using boulders, logs and man-made cover for protection, shade and shelter from the current.

• **Smallmouth are not as weed-oriented as largemouth.** In waters with both weedy and rocky cover, smallmouth are more likely to relate to rocks; largemouth, to weeds. Areas with a combination of weedy and rocky cover often make excellent smallmouth spots and may hold largemouth as well. In lakes with a basin consisting almost entirely of rock, however, smallmouth may seek out sandy, weedy areas because they hold more food.

• **Smallmouth commonly relate to boulders and other large objects.** This tendency is especially noticeable during the spawning period, when smallmouth nest alongside a boulder or log that provides protection from one side. But the fish seek out large objects at other times of the year as well. River smallmouth often rest in the eddy downstream of a large boulder or bridge pier, for example, and lake-dwelling smallmouth commonly seek shade in crevices between boulders, beneath a fallen tree or in a man-made fish shelter.

• **Smallmouth are more likely to suspend in open water than largemouth.** In many deep, clear lakes with large populations of ciscoes or other pelagic (open-water) baitfish, smallmouth commonly feed in open water and may even be caught on the surface over water more than 50 feet deep. From time to time, largemouth also pursue shad and other open-water baitfish, but they are less likely to move away from cover.

• **The best time of day depends mainly on water clarity.** In clear lakes, smallmouth almost always bite best in early morning or around sunset. And in extremely clear lakes, the very best fishing may be at night. In murky or bog-stained lakes, however, the fish usually turn on in mid-day and shut off long before the sun sets.

• **Use the smallmouth's aggressive nature to your benefit.** In waters that have a large smallmouth population, the fish are highly competitive and much more aggressive than they are in waters that hold only a few smallmouth. It's common to hook a smallmouth and see several more following as you reel it in. Some anglers believe the followers are competing for the lure; other say they are merely eating crayfish parts or baitfish that the hooked fish has regurgitated. Be alert for this kind of behavior and be ready to toss another lure at the followers.

In high-competition waters, it's not unusual to hook two smallmouth on the same lure.

The Catch-and-Release Ethic

Because of the smallmouth's reputation as "the gamest fish that swims," the majority of experienced anglers release practically all of the smallmouth they catch. A fish with that much "heart" is worth more on the end of a fishing line than in a frying pan.

But even anglers who throw back every smallmouth they catch often make mistakes that could injure or even kill the fish. Here are some tips that will boost the odds of a successful release:

• Don't use tackle that's too light.

Many smallmouth anglers like to use ultralight tackle in order to get the most fight out of the fish. But in order to land a good-sized smallmouth on ultralight gear, you have to fight it until it is completely exhausted. By that time, so much lactic acid has built up in the bloodstream that the fish's chances of survival are greatly reduced.

• Don't grab the fish by the lower jaw and hold it horizontally.

Even though that's how some of the TV fishing stars do it, holding a smallmouth this way may injure the jaw, especially on a very large fish. If you want to take a picture, hold the fish by the lower jaw (not the gills), but keep its body vertical.

• Release deep-caught fish right away.

When you're hauling fish up from deep water (25 feet or more), the pressure change may cause physical problems. The swim bladder may expand and pop out of the throat or, worse yet, blood vessels may rupture. The problem is most noticeable in fall, when the water temperature is below 50°F.

Fighting a smallmouth on ultralight tackle is a lot of fun, but it's hard on the fish.

The best policy is to leave these deep fish alone, especially during cold-water periods. But if you catch a smallmouth in deep water and want to release it, do it immediately. The longer you keep the fish at the surface, the poorer its chances of surviving.

• If a fish is hooked deep, cut the line.

When you're fishing with live bait, particularly leeches and nightcrawlers, smallmouth will often swallow the bait so deeply that you can't even see your hook. Rather than attempt to remove the hook with a pair of needlenose pliers or a Hookout, just snip the line as close to the hook as possible. This method does not guarantee that the fish will survive, but it vastly increases the odds.

Holding a smallmouth like this may injure its jaw.

When you can't see the hook, just snip the line.

FISHING WITH ARTIFICIALS

You might catch a smallmouth bass on practically any lure you pick off the shelf at your local tackle shop. Like largemouth, smallmouth are versatile feeders, consuming a broad spectrum of fish, crustacean and insect life, and they don't hesitate to bite on any lure that offers a reasonable resemblance.

Nevertheless, you can greatly improve your smallmouth-fishing success by paying attention to the following lure-selection criteria:

Size

As previously explained, smallmouth prefer slightly smaller food items than largemouth, so it's a good idea to use slightly smaller lures.

But that doesn't mean you should never use big lures. In late fall, for example, young-of-the-year baitfish that were only 2 or 3 inches long in July may have grown to a length of 5 inches or more, so a bigger lure is bound to be more effective.

A big minnowbait is a good choice in late fall.

Larger lures also work well for night fishing. A big spinnerbait or topwater makes more commotion and

presents a larger silhouette, almost always drawing more strikes than a smaller, less conspicuous model.

Color

In smallmouth fishing, subtle or natural colors usually outproduce bright or gaudy ones, especially in water that is relatively clear. A crayfish- or baitfish-colored crankbait, for instance, is likely to be much more effective than a fluorescent-colored model. In fact, many anglers have noted that bright colors actually seem to spook smallmouth.

In discolored water, however, bright-colored lures are a plus because they're much easier for the fish to see. While a jig fisherman on a clear lake may prefer a smoke-colored tail, he'll usually pick a white or chartreuse tail when fishing a muddy river.

Action

Just as clearwater smallmouth favor natural colors, they also tend to select a lure with a lifelike action over one with an unrealistic or violent action. This explains why a narrow-lipped minnowbait with a tight rocking action remindful of a lively shiner is a top clearwater-smallmouth pick.

But the natural approach seldom works in low-clarity water. There, you need a lure that moves a lot of water and creates vibrations that the fish can detect using their lateral-line sense. In this situation, a rattlebait (p. 96) or a spinnerbait with a large Colorado blade (p. 100) rank among the very best choices.

Researchers studying smallmouth feeding habits discovered that the fish usually watched their prey closely and then attacked as soon as it stopped moving. This habit has an important implication for smallmouth anglers: Lures that can be fished with an erratic stop-and-go retrieve, such as jerkbaits (p. 107) often catch more fish than those designed to be retrieved steadily.

Here's some advice for selecting and fishing each important kind of smallmouth lure:

TOPWATERS

For sheer smallmouth-fishing excitement, nothing beats a topwater. These surface lures draw explosive strikes from smallmouth in shallow water and, at times, will bring the fish to the surface from depths of 20 feet or more.

Although topwaters are used less for smallmouth than for largemouth, they are no less effective. As a rule, smallmouth prefer smaller topwaters with a more subtle action. Large poppers and other topwaters that make a lot of commotion seem to spook smallmouth.

The very best time for topwaters is in spring, when smallmouth move into the shallows to spawn. But topwaters also catch fish in summer, usually early and late in the day when the fish move into shallow water to feed. In very clear lakes, anglers often use topwaters to "call" smallmouth to the surface after dark.

Weather also plays a role in topwater fishing. Calm, sunny weather warms the water and pulls baitfish into the shallows which, in turn, draw smallmouth into the depth range (5 feet or less) where topwaters are most

effective. Cool, windy weather, on the other hand, keeps baitfish and smallmouth deeper. And even if the fish did move into the shallows, the wave action would make it difficult for them to spot a topwater lure.

Here are the types of topwaters most popular among smallmouth anglers, along with some do's and don'ts for fishing with each of them. Other types of artificials, such as spinnerbaits and floating minnowbaits, can also be used as topwaters, but these lures will be discussed in their respective sections.

How To Catch Smallmouth Bass

PROP-BAITS

Considered by many anglers to be the best topwater for smallmouth, a propbait has a subtle, sputtering action that draws the fishes' attention without spooking them.

Propbaits come in single-blade models that have a propeller at one end or the other, or twin-blade models with propellers at both ends. A single-blade is a good choice in calm water, but a twin-blade throws more water and is easier for the fish to see when the surface is rippled.

Propbaits are normally fished with a twitch-and-pause retrieve. But how hard you twitch and how long you pause depends on the mood

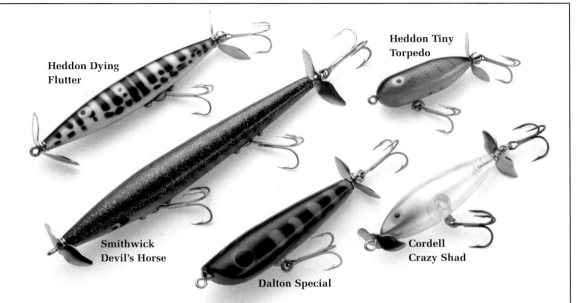

Heddon Dying Flutter

Heddon Tiny Torpedo

Smithwick Devil's Horse

Dalton Special

Cordell Crazy Shad

of the fish. The only sure way to find out is to experiment.

When fishing propbaits and other topwaters as well, most anglers tend to set the hook as soon as they see any kind of splash. But if you set too soon, you'll pull the lure away from the fish. The trick is to hesitate until you actually feel the fish's weight, then set the hook.

Recommended Tackle

For best success with propbaits, use a 6½- to 7-foot medium-heavy power baitcasting rod with a fast tip. Spool up with 10- to 14-pound-test mono and tie the line directly to the lure. Superline is not a good choice for fishing propbaits because it tends to tangle around the front propeller.

Tips for Fishing with Propbaits

Twitch your propbait sharply on a slack line to make it throw water while barely moving forward. This keeps the lure in the fish zone longer.

If you're missing too many strikes, switch to a smaller propbait. Many veteran smallmouth anglers hesitate to use any propbait more than 3 inches long.

Excalibur
Spit'n Image

Excalibur
Super Spook

Mann's Disco Dawg

Berkley
Frenzy Walker

Recommended Tackle

Walking the dog is easiest with a medium-heavy-power, fast-action baitcasting rod no more than 6½ feet long. A longer rod will slap the water on the downward stroke. A stiff rod with a fast tip gives you the sharp twitches necessary to make the lure veer sideways. Spool up with 10- to 14-pound-test mono and tie the line directly to the lure.

STICKBAITS

Stickbaits resemble propbaits, although they lack the propeller blades. But there's another important difference: A stickbait has a weight in the tail so it floats with its head up. This makes it possible to "walk the dog," using a series of rapid downward twitches of the rod so the lure veers erratically from side to side.

This retrieve mimics an injured minnow and often draws smallmouth from a considerable distance. It can also be used to call them up from the depths.

Walking the dog has another big advantage: Because you're retrieving quite rapidly, you can cover more water in a shorter time than you can with a propbait.

Although stickbaits have great fish-attracting power, they do not make a lot of commotion. Consequently, they work best in clear, calm water; they are much less effective in muddy or choppy water.

Tips for Fishing with Stickbaits

Tune a stickbait just as you would a crankbait if it's veering to one side. If it veers to the left, for example, bend the attachment eye to the right and vice versa. Or, you can intentionally mistune a normal stickbait to make it veer under a dock, an overhanging limb or other overhead cover.

When a smallmouth strikes at your stickbait but misses it, you may tend to slow down your retrieve so the fish can "catch up." But that's almost always a mistake. Instead, keep the lure moving at the same speed until you complete the retrieve.

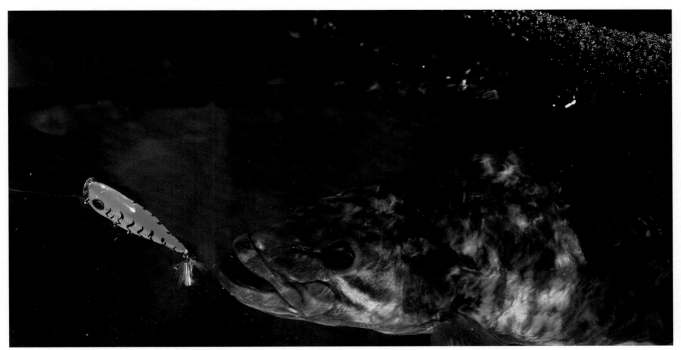

Sometimes you have to pause between twitches long enough for the ripples to subside.

CHUGGERS

Even in the muddiest water, smallmouth can easily hear and track the sound of a chugger. But a big chugger that makes a loud splashing noise is more likely to scare off smallmouth than attract them. In most cases, they prefer a smaller lure with a more subdued action.

Chuggers are sometimes called poppers because the face catches water and makes a popping sound when you twitch the lure. Chuggers with a scooped-out face catch more water and make a louder popping sound than those with a flattened face.

Chuggers, like stickbaits, are usually retrieved with a series of rapid twitches. But there will be times when you'll have better success by twitching and then pausing for a few seconds before twitching again. How hard you twitch and how long you pause depends on the mood of the bass, but gentle twitches almost always work better than violent ones.

When you make a cast and start your retrieve, hold your rod tip fairly high at first, in order to keep your line from sinking and pulling the nose of the lure under. Gradually lower your rod at the end of your retrieve so you don't pull the lure's nose out of the water.

Recommended Tackle

Chuggers are relatively light so you'll need a rod with a fairly soft tip to cast them. A 6½-foot medium-power, medium-action baitcaster is a good all-around choice. Spool up with 10- to 14-pound-test mono and tie the line directly to the lure.

Rebel Pop'R

Storm Chug Bug

Berkley Frenzy Popper

Rapala Skitter Pop

Bassmex Pop-a-Top

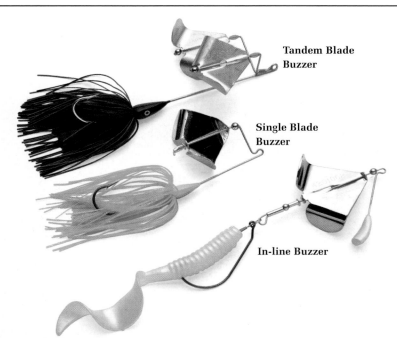

Tandem Blade Buzzer

Single Blade Buzzer

In-line Buzzer

surface disturbance. A straight-shaft buzzer will give you a higher hooking percentage, but you'll need a safety-pin shaft for fishing in weedy cover.

To get the best action from a buzzbait, hold your rod tip high at the beginning of the retrieve to keep the lure riding level and the blade spinning freely. Reel steadily and just rapidly enough to keep the lure on the surface. Gradually lower your rod during the retrieve; otherwise, you'll pull the nose of the lure out of the water so the blade can't spin.

BUZZBAITS

Although buzzbaits are mainly considered to be largemouth lures, they work equally well for smallmouth. Because "buzzers" throw a lot of water and make a loud gurgling sound, they're a good choice in discolored water, at night or when the surface is rippled.

Like stickbaits, buzzbaits can be retrieved rapidly, so they work well in situations where you want to cover a lot of water to find fish. But with such a fast retrieve, you may get a lot of short strikes. If this happens, switch to a different kind of surface lure to catch the fish you've located.

Buzzbaits come in single- and tandem-blade models with either a straight or safety-pin shaft. Single-blade models usually work best for smallmouth because they have a smaller profile and create less

Recommended Tackle

A 7½-foot flippin' stick is a good choice for buzzbait fishing because it helps you make long casts. The extra length also makes it easy to keep your rod tip high so the lure rides level at the beginning of the retrieve. Use a reel with a gear ratio of at least 6:1 for a fast retrieve, and spool up with 14- to 17-pound-test mono. Tie the line directly to the lure.

Buzzbaiting Tips

Make extra-long casts when fishing with buzz-baits. This covers more water and gives the fish more time to "track" the lure.

When you're fishing in open water and small-mouth are striking short, slip a piece of surgical tubing over the shank of a treble hook and then push the eye of the treble over the buzzbait hook.

How To Catch Smallmouth Bass

Crawlers make a distinct gurgling sound as they swim across the surface.

CRAWLERS

Because crawlers make more commotion than other kinds of topwaters, they're not a particularly good choice for smallmouth in most situations. But like buzzbaits, they can be quite effective at night or under other low-visibility conditions such as choppy or murky water. Another similarity: Crawlers are normally fished by making long casts and rapid retrieves, so they make good "locator" lures.

Crawlers have one big advantage over buzzbaits, however. Crawlers float rather than sink when at rest, so they can also be fished with a stop-and-go retrieve. There will be some times when smallmouth ignore a lure retrieved steadily, but strike when it pauses for a few seconds.

The crawling action and gurgling sound of these lures is produced by either a wide faceplate or a pair of hinged "arms." Faceplate models are usually the best choice for smallmouth because their action is not as intense. They also work better in weedy cover because the faceplate doesn't pick up as many weeds as the arms.

The tackle recommended for fishing buzzbaits also works well for fishing crawlers. Always tie the line directly to the lure.

Arbogast Jitterbug

Arbogast Jointed Jitterbug

Heddon Creeper

CRANKBAITS

Smallmouth find it hard to resist a crankbait bumping along the bottom and kicking up clouds of silt. The action probably resembles that of a crayfish scooting for cover. In fact, you'll find a good selection of crayfish-pattern crankbaits in the tackle box of practically every serious smallmouth angler.

Besides color, the main considerations in selecting crankbaits are running depth and action. You can buy crankbaits in shallow-, medium- and deep-running models, and it's a good idea to carry a few of each for fishing in different water depths. Some shallow runners track at a depth of less than 5 feet, while some deep divers reach depths of more than 20 feet.

If you're not sure whether a plug runs shallow or deep, take a look at the lip. A long lip that is in line with the horizontal axis of the body means that the plug is a deep diver. A short lip angled sharply down from the horizontal axis makes it a shallow runner.

Exactly what type of action a crankbait has depends on the shape of the lip and body. In general, a crankbait with a narrow lip and thin body has a tight wiggle; one with a broad lip and fat body, a wide wobble.

The majority of crankbaits are floaters, although some models sink and others are neutrally buoyant. While the running depth of a floater is pretty much fixed, a sinker can be fished at a variety of depths by counting it down before starting your retrieve. Neutrally buoyant crankbaits can be fished very slowly or even stopped in mid-retrieve without floating up or sinking.

Most crankbait fishermen prefer monofilament line because the stretch allows a fish to take the lure deeper. But switching to superline, which has only a fraction of the diameter, allows a crankbait to run 30 to 50 percent deeper. Superline is also becoming more popular among crankbait trollers. If you do use superline, however, choose a soft-tipped rod to compensate for the lack of line stretch.

Recommended Tackle

A 6½- to 7½-foot, long-handled baitcasting rod with a soft tip is a good choice for crankbait fishing. It enables you to make long casts and prevents you from setting the hook too soon, pulling the lure away from the fish. Pair it with a high-gear-ratio reel (at least 5:1) and spool up with 12- to 20-pound-test mono. For maximum wiggle, attach the lure to the line using a split ring or round-nosed snap.

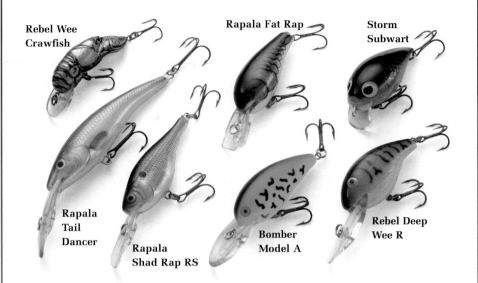

Rebel Wee Crawfish

Rapala Fat Rap

Storm Subwart

Rapala Tail Dancer

Rapala Shad Rap RS

Bomber Model A

Rebel Deep Wee R

How to Retrieve a Crankbait

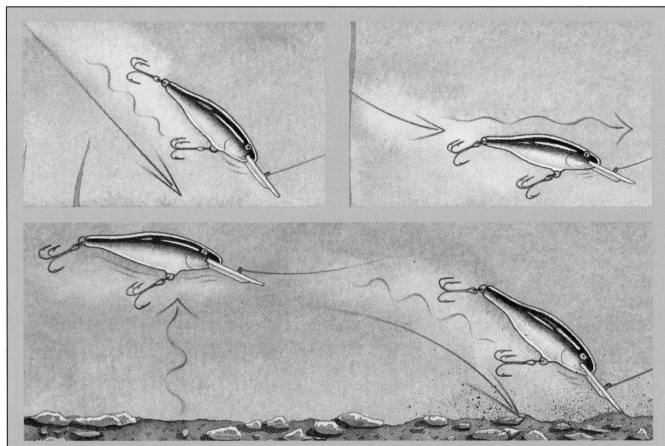

Make an extra-long cast so the lure lands well past the expected fish zone. To get the lure down to its maximum running depth, crank rapidly at first (top left) and then slow down as the lure comes through the fish zone (top right). If desired, try a stop-and-go retrieve (bottom), pausing to let the lure float up a little and then reeling rapidly to draw it down and bump bottom. The erratic action usually triggers more strikes than a steady retrieve.

MINNOWBAITS

Many anglers fail to make the distinction between minnowbaits and crankbaits. To them, any subsurface lure that has a lip is a "crankbait." But there are important differences that can affect your smallmouth-fishing success.

• Minnowbaits have a long, thin body and a lifelike swimming action that more closely resembles that of the thin-bodied baitfish, such as shiner minnows, that smallmouth favor.

• The realistic look of a minnowbait makes it a better choice than a crankbait in clear water. But because its action is more subtle, a minnowbait does not work as well as a crankbait in murky water.

• Minnowbaits have better action than crankbaits on a slow retrieve, so they're a better choice in cool water.

Like crankbaits, minnowbaits come in a wide variety of models designed to run at different depths. Most are floaters, but some sink slowly and others, called jerkbaits, are neutrally buoyant.

Floating minnowbaits work best with a slow, steady retrieve. They aren't well suited to a stop-and-go retrieve because their high buoyancy makes them float up rapidly when you pause. But floaters are deadly when fished on the surface using a twitch-and-pause retrieve. They dart down and wiggle when you twitch, then float up lifelessly when you pause, making a near-perfect imitation of an injured minnow (opposite).

A jerkbait fished with a stop-and-go retrieve will often trigger strikes from finicky smallmouth.

Sinkers are a good choice for fishing in deep water because you can count them down to any depth. But the internal weight reduces their action, so they don't have as much wiggle as floaters.

Jerkbaits rank among the hottest new smallmouth lures. They work especially well when cool water or adverse weather conditions make the fish sluggish. Even if they're not in a chasing mood, they'll often grab a jerkbait hanging right in their face (above).

Recommended Tackle

Floating minnowbaits are notoriously difficult to cast because they are light and wind-resistant. But casting will be easier if you use a long spinning rod with a soft tip that flexes easily on the backcast. A long-spool spinning reel spooled with 6- to 8-pound-test limp monofilament will also improve casting performance. You can tie your minnowbait directly to the line or attach it with a loop knot or small round-nosed clip.

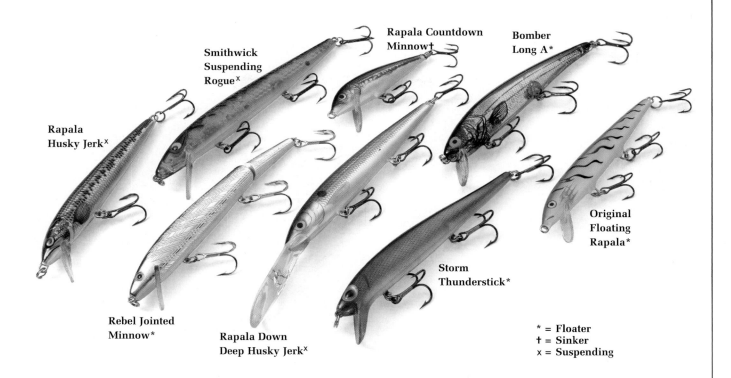

Rapala
Husky Jerk[x]

Smithwick
Suspending
Rogue[x]

Rapala Countdown
Minnow[†]

Bomber
Long A[*]

Rebel Jointed
Minnow[*]

Rapala Down
Deep Husky Jerk[x]

Storm
Thunderstick[*]

Original
Floating
Rapala[*]

[*] = Floater
[†] = Sinker
[x] = Suspending

How to Use a Floating Minnowbait as a Topwater

Make a sharp downward twitch with your rod tip to make the minnowbait dart beneath the surface.

Pause for a few seconds to allow the lure to float back up to the surface, and then let it settle to rest before twitching again. Smallmouth usually strike when the lure is motionless.

VIBRATING PLUGS

The tight wiggling action of these subsurface plugs often triggers strikes from smallmouth that ignore plugs with a "looser" swimming action. Vibrating plugs work especially well in discolored water, where the fish can detect the intense vibrations using their lateral-line sense. Many vibrating plugs, called "rattlebaits" have internal beads to create even more commotion.

Sometimes called "lipless crankbaits," these lures have a thin body, a flat forehead and no lip. The tight wiggle is created by the force of water against the forehead.

Because vibrating plugs have no lip to make them dive, most models are designed to sink. This means you can fish practically any depth of water simply by counting the lure down before starting your retrieve.

Vibrating plugs make excellent "search" lures. Because they are heavily weighted and have an aerodynamic shape, you can cast them a long distance. And they work best with a rapid retrieve, so you can cover a lot of water in a short time to find the active feeders.

Yet another big advantage: Vibrating plugs work well for calling smallmouth out of submerged weeds because there is no lip to catch vegetation. Just cast the lure out, count it down to the right level and start your retrieve. If you feel the lure bumping the weedtops, just hold your rod tip a little higher and reel a little faster. After a few casts, you'll learn exactly what count and retrieve speed works best to keep the lure right above the weedtops (opposite).

Recommended Tackle

Fishing with vibrating plugs involves long casts and fast retrieves, so it pays to use a long-handled, medium-heavy-power baitcasting rod from 6½ to 7 feet in length and a high-speed baitcasting reel spooled with 10- to 14-pound-test mono. Always attach your lure with a small snap or a loop knot for maximum wiggle.

Cordell
Super Spot

Berkley
Frenzy Rattl'r

Bill Lewis
Rat-L-Trap

Rapala
Rattlin' Rap

Blinky

How to Work a Weedy Break with a Vibrating Plug

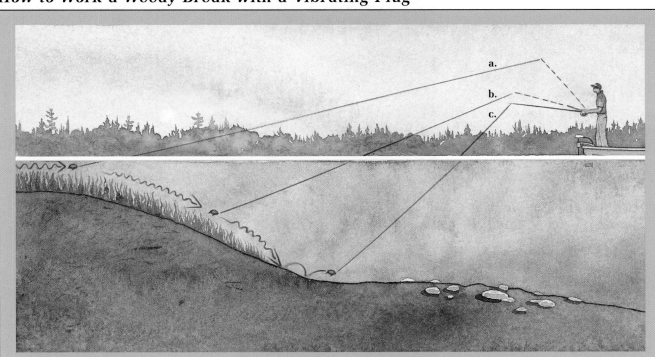

With your boat positioned over deep water, make a long cast into the shallows and (a) start reeling as soon as the lure hits the water. Keep your rod tip high and adjust your retrieve speed to keep the lure just above the weedtops. When the lure reaches the break, (b) gradually slow down your retrieve and drop your rod tip so the lure tracks deeper and deeper. When the bottom flattens out, (c) lower your rod and slow down your retrieve even more, allowing the lure to periodically bump bottom.

SPINNERS

Although spinners don't get much press, you'll find a good selection of them in the tackle boxes of most veteran smallmouth anglers. Not only are spinners one of the easiest lures to use, their combination of flash and vibration has top-notch smallmouth appeal.

You can use spinners in practically any kind of smallmouth water, but they work best in current. There, you can pull the lure up to a rock, log or other likely piece of cover and pause to let it "hang" in place while the current turns the blades and prevents the lure from sinking.

You can choose from two main types of spinners:

• **French Spinner.** In this type, the blades rotate around the shaft on a U-shaped metal attachment called a *clevis*. French spinners emit intense vibrations, making them a good choice in discolored water.

• **Sonic Spinner.** These lures have a unique blade designed to catch water and spin easily. This means they can be retrieved very slowly or allowed to "hang" in slow current. The blade, which is concave on one end and convex on the other, spins directly on the shaft rather than on a clevis. Sonic spinners produce less vibration than French spinners, so they work best in relatively clear water.

Both types of spinners have an exposed hook, so they are not a good choice for fishing in dense weeds or brush. There, you'll have better success with a spinnerbait or other lure with a protected hook. Another consideration: If you tie a spinner

How To Catch Smallmouth Bass

directly to your line, it will spin on the retrieve and cause serious line twist. But you can easily avoid the problem by attaching the spinner with a ball-bearing swivel or by bending the front of the shaft at a 45-degree angle.

In most cases, there is no need to tip your spinner with live bait. But when fishing is tough, some anglers add a minnow, small leech or piece of nightcrawler for scent appeal.

Recommended Tackle

Casting these lightweight lures is easiest with a medium-power spinning outfit with a fairly light tip. If your rod is too stiff, it won't flex or "load" on the backcast, so you'll have to throw the lure rather than letting the rod do the work. A wide-spool spinning reel filled with 4- to 8-pound mono also improves casting performance.

* = French spinner
† = Sonic spinner

Mepp's Black Fury*

Blue Fox Minnow Spin*

Mepp's Thunderbug*

Panther Martin†

Sonic Rooster Tail†

Tips for Using Spinners

When wade-fishing for stream smallmouth, stand upstream of key spots and use a long rod to guide your spinner into small eddies. This way, you can fish several pockets without moving your feet, which would stir up silt and disturb the fish.

Tip your spinner with a small pork strip for extra attraction. The pork not only wiggles enticingly, it provides a little extra lift, enabling you to slow your retrieve without the lure sinking to the bottom and hanging up.

SPINNERBAITS

Most fishermen think of spinnerbaits as largemouth lures, but they work equally well for smallmouth. Among the most versatile of bass lures, spinnerbaits are a good choice in a wide variety of situations.

Because the hook is protected by the safety-pin shaft, a spinnerbait will track through light to moderate vegetation without fouling. But spinnerbaits can also be fished in open water and counted down to most any depth.

Spinnerbaits also have some special applications. The blade "helicopters" as the lure sinks, slowing the sink rate and giving bass more time to strike. Helicoptering works especially well for fishing vertical cover, such as a cliff face or a submerged tree

trunk. And it enables you to use an erratic stop-and-go retrieve, reeling steadily for a few seconds and then hesitating to let the lure helicopter before resuming your retrieve.

You can also fish a spinnerbait by jigging it along the bottom, "slow-rolling" it over cover, "bulging" it on the surface by holding your rod tip high and reeling just fast enough to make it push a little water, or sputtering it on

the surface by reeling a little faster so the blades actually break water.

There are two main styles of spinnerbaits. A *single-spin* emits a strong beat and is the best choice for helicoptering. A *tandem-spin* has a pair of blades on the upper arm, giving it more lift so it can be retrieved very slowly without sinking into the cover.

Another consideration in selecting spinnerbaits is the

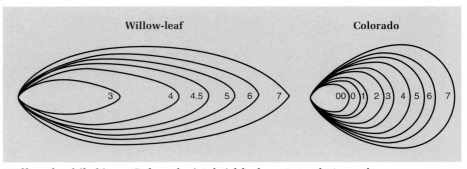

Willow-leaf (left) vs. Colorado (right) blades. Actual sizes shown.

blade style. Colorado and willow-leaf blades are the most common, with the wider Colorado blades giving you the most lift and vibration.

They work best for slow retrieves and helicoptering, and their strong beat makes them a good choice in murky water. The narrower willow-leaf blades present a more realistic baitfish-like profile and, because the blades spin closer to the shaft, they aren't as likely to foul in vegetation.

Recommended Tackle

A 6½-foot medium-power bait-casting rod and a high-speed baitcasting reel spooled with 12- to 17-pound-test mono makes a good all-around spinnerbait outfit. If you'll be doing a lot of distance casting, choose a long-handled rod for extra casting leverage. Always tie the line directly to the lure.

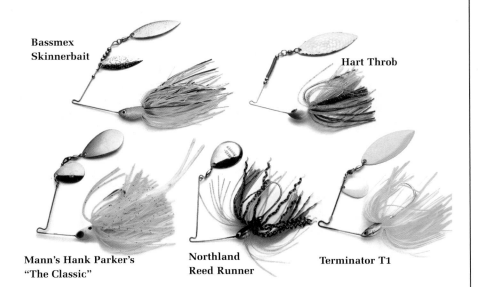

Bassmex Skinnerbait

Hart Throb

Mann's Hank Parker's "The Classic"

Northland Reed Runner

Terminator T1

Popular Spinnerbait Retrieves

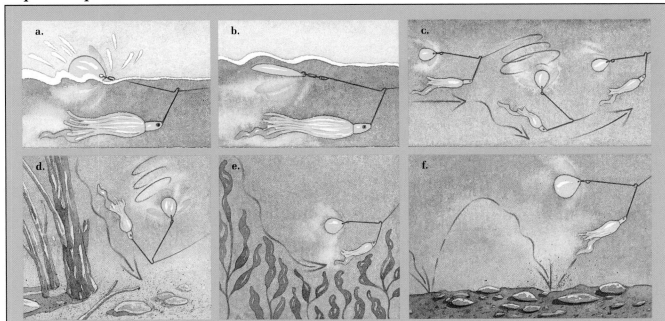

Retrieve a spinnerbait by (a) keeping your rod tip high and reeling rapidly to make the blades break the surface; (b) keeping your rod tip high and reeling a little slower so the blades bulge the surface; (c) using a stop-and-go retrieve in open water, letting the lure helicopter on the pause; (d) helicopter-ing the lure down vertical cover; (e) slow-rolling the lure by reeling slowly to follow the contour of logs, brush, weeds or other cover; (f) using a lift-and-drop retrieve to jig the lure along the bottom.

SOFT PLASTICS

Experienced smallmouth anglers know that the natural look of soft-plastic baits will often catch fish when conditions are tough. In super-clear water, for example, where the fish can closely examine your offering, the wiggling tentacles of a soft-plastic tubebait often draw strikes from smallmouth that ignore other kinds of lures.

Another big advantage of soft plastics: They have a lifelike texture, so when a smallmouth grabs the lure, it will usually hold on long enough to give you time to set the hook.

Soft plastics are an excellent choice for fishing in dense cover because they can be rigged Texas-style (p. 103).

With the hook point buried in the plastic, you can drag them through the heaviest weeds or brush without hanging up or fouling.

When selecting soft-plastic lures, many anglers make the mistake of focusing too much on style and color, and not enough on the texture and hardness of the material. If the plastic is too hard, it will not only have an unnatural look but also an unnatural feel. If the plastic is too soft, it will have a gummy texture and the legs or tentacles may actually stick to the body or tear off under the slightest pressure. And if you try to rig the bait Texas-style, the hook point won't stay imbedded in

the body. In most cases, soft plastics of intermediate hardness are the best choice.

Recommended Tackle

For smaller soft plastics (up to 4" long), use a 6- to 6$\frac{1}{2}$-foot medium-power spinning outfit with 6- to 8-pound-test mono. For larger soft plastics, you'll probably need a 6- to 6$\frac{1}{2}$-foot medium-heavy-power baitcasting outfit with 12- to 17-pound-test mono. Soft plastics are almost always tied directly to your line, with no clips or snaps.

CRAWS

As much as smallmouth love to eat crayfish, it's not surprising that soft-plastic "craws" make excellent smallmouth baits.

There are two basic types of craws: semi-realistic models that have a worm-like body with pincers on the end, and ultra-realistic models that are molded to mimic a real crayfish.

Semi-realistic craws are by far the most popular. They can be fished on a plain worm hook rigged Texas-style or Carolina-style (below left), or used to tip a jig or spinnerbait. Always rig the lure with the pincers trailing so it resembles a real crayfish jetting backwards to escape a predator.

Ultra-realistic craws, though used less commonly, can be a great choice in very clear water. Some models have so much detail that it's difficult to distinguish them from the real thing. They're normally rigged by pushing a hook through the back and out the snout (below right).

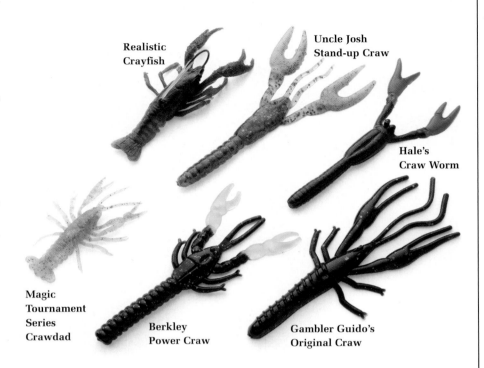

Realistic Crayfish

Uncle Josh Stand-up Craw

Hale's Craw Worm

Magic Tournament Series Crawdad

Berkley Power Craw

Gambler Guido's Original Craw

How to Rig Soft-Plastic Craws

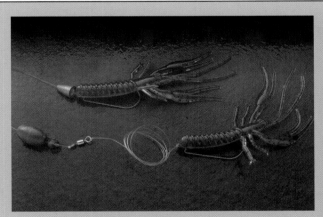

Texas-rig a semi-realistic craw by pushing a worm hook into the narrow end, threading it through about ¼ inch, then turning the hook and pushing it just about, but not quite, all the way through the body. Add a bullet sinker for weight (top). Or, make a Carolina rig (bottom) by threading an egg sinker and bead onto your line, adding a barrel swivel and then tying on a 2- to 3-foot leader. On a clean bottom, you can fish a Carolina rig with the hook exposed.

Rig an ultra-realistic craw by pushing a worm hook into the back just in front of the tail, threading it through the entire body and then bringing it out the snout with the point up. If necessary, add a split-shot or two 12 to 18 inches up the line.

The tentacles of a tubebait wiggle enticingly when you shake your rod tip.

TUBEBAITS

The popularity of tubebaits, known simply as "tubes," is growing rapidly among smallmouth addicts. That's because the fish find it hard to resist the enticing wiggle of the tentacles.

As its name suggests, a tubebait is merely a hollow soft-plastic tube with the rear half sliced into thin strips resembling the tentacles of a squid. Tubebaits can be rigged with a worm hook and bullet sinker (Texas-style or exposed) or fished on a specially designed tube hook with a clip that prevents the body from sliding back and an internal weight (opposite). Another option is to rig a tube with an internal jig head (p. 111).

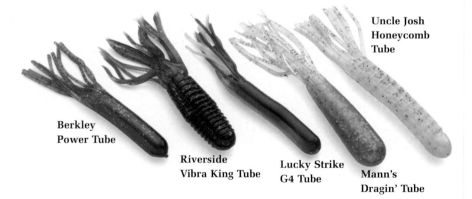

Berkley
Power Tube

Riverside
Vibra King Tube

Lucky Strike
G4 Tube

Mann's
Dragin' Tube

Uncle Josh
Honeycomb
Tube

The beauty of a tubebait is that it can be fished very slowly yet retain good action. In fact, one effective method is jiggling the bait in place by rapidly shaking your rod tip without retrieving line. This method works especially well for sight fishing (p. 148).

Most tubes used for smallmouth are 3 to 4 inches in length, although there are times when larger ones work better. In fall, for instance, fishermen sometimes use 5- or 6-inchers to match the size of young-of-the-year baitfish.

Weedless Rigging Method with Internal Weight

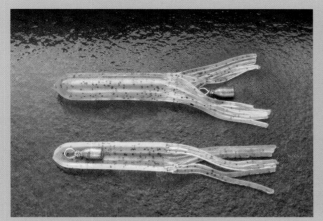

1 *Drop a specially designed tube weight down the inside of the tube so the ring rests at the head of the bait.*

2 *Push the point of an Eagle Claw HP hook into the head of the bait, through the sinker ring and out the side.*

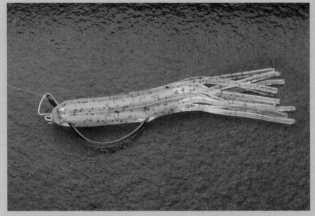

3 *Give the hook a half turn, push the eye through the nose, and push the point through the side so it barely protrudes.*

4 *Attach the wire clip to the hook shank to prevent the tube from sliding back.*

Exposed Hook Rigging Method

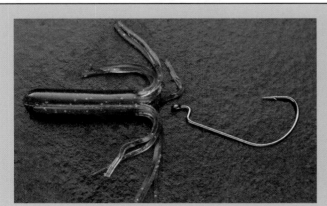

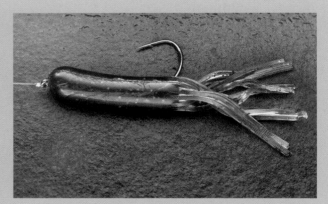

Push a straight-shank worm hook through the back end of the tube (left) and continue pushing until the hook eye pokes out the nose of the tube (right). Add a bullet sinker for weight or use a Carolina rig.

WORMS & LIZARDS

Although plastic worms and lizards are used less frequently for smallmouth than for largemouth, they definitely have their place in a smallmouth angler's arsenal.

When the fish are buried in weeds or brush, for example, a Texas-rigged worm will snake through the tangle with few problems. And a lizard is a good choice at spawning time, probably because the fish see it as a threat to their nest.

When smallmouth are on a clean bottom, a Carolina rig with an exposed hook usually works better than a Texas rig. Not only does the exposed hook improve your hooking percentage, you'll probably get more strikes because the lure settles to the bottom more slowly. Another good way to rig these baits on a clean bottom: Simply pinch on a split-shot about a foot up the line.

While largemouth fishermen rely mainly on worms and lizards from 6 to 10 inches long, most smallmouth anglers favor baits in the 4- to 7-inch range.

Besides length, other important considerations in selecting these baits include the hardness of the plastic and the type of tail.

If you'll be rigging Texas-style, a softer-bodied bait is the best choice so the hook point can easily penetrate the plastic on the hookset. But if you're using a Carolina rig with an exposed hook, a harder-bodied bait is more durable and will last longer.

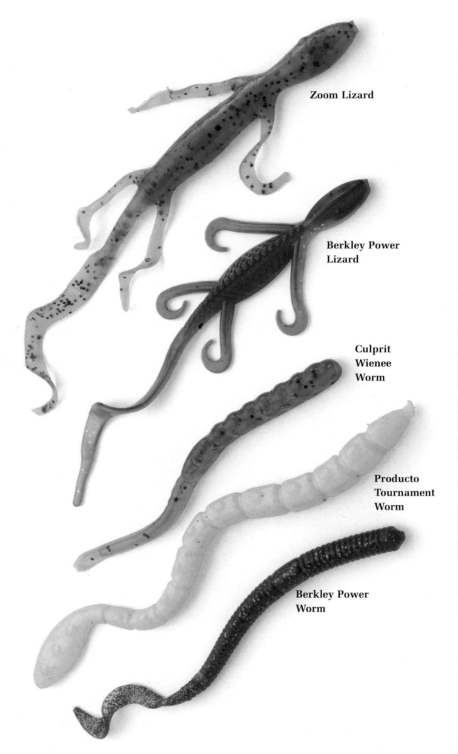

Zoom Lizard

Berkley Power Lizard

Culprit Wienee Worm

Producto Tournament Worm

Berkley Power Worm

Most lizards come with a curly tail, but worms are available in a variety of tail styles. Curly tails are quite popular because they have the most action. But there are times when the fish prefer paddletails, which have a slower throbbing action, or straight-tails, which have no action other than what the angler imparts.

SOFT JERKBAITS

When shallow-water small-mouth are in a finicky mood, it's hard to beat a soft jerkbait. The bait sinks very slowly, so you can hang it right in the fish's face.

Soft jerkbaits have no action of their own; you impart the action by retrieving with downward jerks followed by pauses that allow the lure to glide sideways in a horizontal position. Fished properly, the lure will "walk" from side to side with an erratic, wounded-baitfish action.

Soft jerkbaits are normally fished with no weight, but

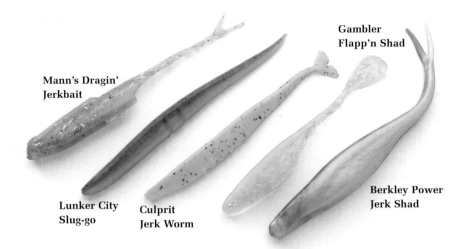

Mann's Dragin' Jerkbait

Gambler Flapp'n Shad

Lunker City Slug-go

Culprit Jerk Worm

Berkley Power Jerk Shad

you can push a small lead insert or a nail into the body to make the lure cast a little farther and run a little deeper (below).

Most smallmouth anglers prefer 4-inch jerkbaits, but 6-inchers may work better when the fish are feeding on large baitfish.

How to Rig Soft Jerkbaits

1 Push an offset worm hook into the bait as far as the offset.

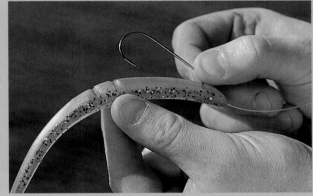

2 Bring the point out the bottom and turn the hook 180 degrees.

3 Push the hook point through the body so it rests in the depression on the back.

4 If desired, push a lead insert or finishing nail into the body just ahead of the hook bend.

JIGS

No smallmouth box would be complete without a good selection of leadhead jigs. You can choose from dozens of different types of leadheads, but the following are most popular in smallmouth-fishing circles:

• **Jig/Grub Combo.** An ordinary round-head jig tipped with a soft-plastic grub such as a curlytail, shad-tail or paddletail is the "old standard" among veteran smallmouth anglers.

• **Fly 'n' Rind.** A hair or feather jig tipped with pork rind is the top choice of many southern smallmouth experts. The hair or feather dressing gives the jig a pulsating or "breathing" action.

• **Tube Jig.** A specially designed tube head inside of a soft-plastic tubebait gives this lure an ultra-realistic look.

• **Jig 'n' Pig.** With its weedguard and bullet-shaped head, this jig will come through the heaviest cover without hanging up or collecting weeds. The jig is normally tipped with a pork trailer, but soft plastic trailers are also popular.

• **Jig Worm.** This bait consists of a mushroom-head jig tipped with a plastic worm. Because the plastic butts up against the flattened surface of the head, the lure has a very natural look and no groove between the head and body to collect weeds.

One of the most important considerations in selecting jigs is weight. As a rule, you should use the lightest jig that will still get to the bottom, considering wind velocity and current speed.

A slow-sinking jig is a must in smallmouth fishing.

Smallmouth, like most other gamefish, usually hit a jig while it is sinking; a light jig gives you a slower sink rate so the fish have more time to strike.

The usual formula for calculating jig weight is to allow 1/8 ounce for every 10 feet of depth. But if you're fishing in a strong crosswind or a swift current, you may have to double or triple that weight.

On the following pages, you'll find details on rigging and fishing each of the important jig types.

Recommended Tackle

Jig strikes may be very subtle, so you'll need a sensitive, high-modulus graphite rod with a fast tip to detect them. In light cover, most smallmouth anglers use a medium-power spinning outfit spooled with 6- to 10-pound-test mono. In heavier cover, you'll need a medium- to medium-heavy-power baitcasting outfit with 10- to 17-pound-test mono. Always tie your line directly to the jig.

Paddletail   **Squidtail**   **Crawfish**   **Curlytail**   **Shadtail**   **Soft Plastic/ Marabou**

JIG/GRUB COMBO

A jig and grub is an excellent choice for fishing a clean rocky, gravelly or sandy bottom, but the open hook would quickly hang up in woody cover. You can "rip" a jig and grub through cabbage and other crispy-leaved vegetation, but stringy weeds will soon gather on the hook and attachment eye.

The seductive action of a curlytail grub makes it the best all-around choice for tipping a jig, but there are times when other kinds of trailers work better. A shadtail, for instance, usually works well in rivers or reservoirs with a shad forage base. And a paddletail, with its more subtle action, is worth a try when the fish are not feeding aggressively. Other tipping possibilities include small craws, lizards and worms.

How to Rig a Jig and Grub

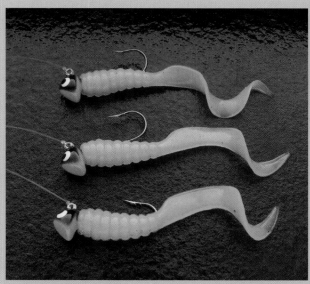

Curlytail. Push a curlytail onto the hook far enough to cover the entire shank up to the bend (top). If you don't push it on far enough, the grub won't ride straight and may tear off the hook (middle). If you push the grub on too far, it will wrap around the hook bend and look unnatural (bottom).

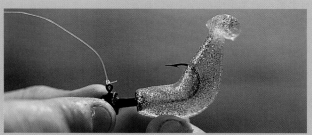

Shadtail. Push the hook through a shadtail far enough to cover the entire shank up to the bend. Then bring the hook out the back of the grub.

Paddletail. These tails can be rigged either horizontally (top) or vertically (bottom). Either way, push the hook through the tail far enough to cover the entire shank up to the bend.

The billowing action and slow sink rate of a fly 'n' rind is a deadly smallmouth combination.

FLY 'N' RIND

You can tip most any kind of a hair or feather jig with a pork trailer to make a fly 'n' rind. If you'll be fishing on a relatively clean bottom, choose a jig with an unprotected hook. In heavy cover, you'll need a jig with a bullet-shaped head and a bristle, wire or plastic weedguard.

The pork trailer not only gives the lure a lifelike look, the extra bulk greatly slows the sink rate, giving the fish more time to strike. Although pork frogs and split-tail eels are the most popular kinds of pork trailers, a wide variety of other pork "products" are now available, including craws, waterdogs, leeches and Ripple Rind. You can also buy a variety of soft-plastic trailers that are impregnated with pork and scent.

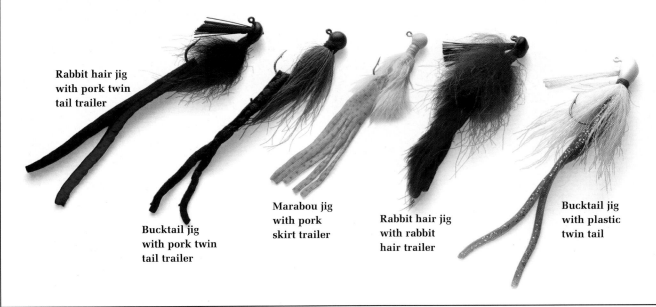

Rabbit hair jig with pork twin tail trailer

Bucktail jig with pork twin tail trailer

Marabou jig with pork skirt trailer

Rabbit hair jig with rabbit hair trailer

Bucktail jig with plastic twin tail

How To Catch Smallmouth Bass

TUBE JIG

Tube jigs are usually regarded as clear-water lures, because they do not create the vibration necessary to attract smallmouth in discolored water. Like jig-and-grub combos, tube jigs work best on a relatively clean bottom.

A tube jig consists of a soft-plastic tubebait rigged on a jig head. The majority of tubebaits have a hollow body, so they must be rigged with an internal, cylindrical-shaped jig head (below). With an ordinary jig head, the hollow tube would slip back on the hook shank.

But a few tubebaits have a solid body, meaning that they can be rigged on an external jig head with the body held in place by the barbed collar.

How to Rig Tube Jigs

Internal Jig Head. *Insert a tube head into the opening of a tubebait (top). Push the head to the front of the tube and then poke the eye through the plastic (bottom).*

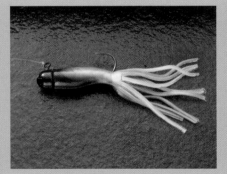

External Jig Head. *Push a solid-bodied tubebait onto a jig head, preferably a mushroom head, with a strongly barbed collar. With a mushroom head, there is no gap between the head and the tube to gather weeds.*

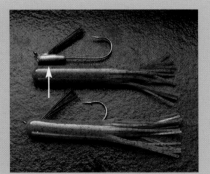

Weedless Rig. *Select a tube head with a weedguard, then hold it against the tubebait to determine where the weedguard will protrude (arrow, top). Push the hook through the tube at that point and then push the head into the front of the tube, leaving only the weedguard exposed (bottom).*

Jig 'N' Pig

Whether you call it a jig 'n' pig or a pig 'n' jig, this versatile lure is a favorite of anglers probing for bass in dense cover. Besides having a bristle or plastic weedguard, most of these jigs have a bullet- or cone-shaped head with the attachment eye at the tip, so they slide easily through weeds, timber, brush and other kinds of heavy cover. Most models have an extra-heavy hook that won't bend when you horse fish out of the tangle.

As their name implies, these jigs are normally tipped with some kind of pork product, usually a frog or eel, so they sink fairly slowly. Some anglers, however, prefer soft-plastic trailers, particularly curlytails and craws. Most of these jigs also have a live-rubber or silicone skirt, which is usually reversed to add bulk and slow the sink rate even more.

Heavy cover situations often call for a jig 'n' pig.

How to Rig a Jig 'n' Pig

Pork Trailer. *Push the hook through the prepunched hole in a pork frog or eel, from the bottom up.*

Soft-Plastic Trailer. *Add a curlytail (top) or a craw (bottom) by pushing it onto the hook far enough to cover the entire shank up to the bend.*

Ripping a jig worm off the weeds creates an extreme darting action that gets a smallmouth's attention.

JIG WORM

For fishing in sparse weeds or working a weedline, it's tough to beat a jig worm. Although the lure has an exposed hook that will occasionally pick up weeds, the thin-diameter shank usually rips through the vegetation when you give the bait a sharp tug.

You can thread a plastic worm on any kind of jig head, but the best jig worms have a mushroom head with a flattened rear surface. This way, when you push the worm flush against the head, there is very little, if any, gap to collect bits of weeds, stringy algae or other debris. Most mushroom heads have a double-barbed collar to hold the worm firmly. The mushroom head also gives the lure an unusual action. When you

snap it off a weed, the lure darts upward erratically and then sinks back down slowly, drawing more strikes than an ordinary round-head jig.

Most smallmouth anglers tip their jigs with 4- to 6-inch worms, usually curlytails. Longer worms result in too many short strikes.

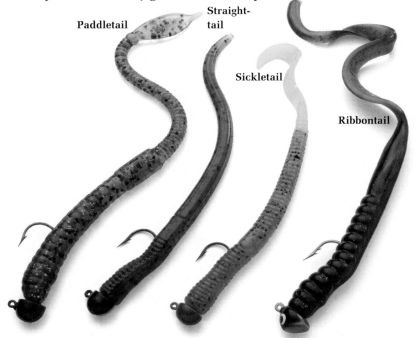

JIGGING LURES

Jigging lures don't get much press, but smallmouth insiders know how effective they can be. Although they're not widely used among northcountry anglers, they've long been popular among Southern smallmouth addicts.

Jigging lures differ from leadhead jigs in that they have some kind of built-in action. There are three main types:

• **Bladebaits.** With their thin metal body and lead head, these lures vibrate rapidly when pulled upward but have little action on the drop. They are sometimes called "vibrating blades."

• **Jigging Spoons.** These thick metal spoons sink rapidly and have an erratic tumbling action when jigged vertically. Because of their heavy weight, they also work well for distance casting.

• **Tailspins.** These lures have a heavy lead body with a single spinner blade on the tail that turns on both the lift and the drop. They are used for both vertical jigging and distance casting.

All three types of jigging lures are relatively heavy for their size, so they are good for working deep-water structure or fishing in current. But many anglers make the mistake of selecting jigging lures that are *too* heavy. As in fishing leadhead jigs, the idea is to use the lightest lure that will easily reach the desired depth.

Here are specifics on fishing with each of these lure types:

Recommended Tackle

A medium-heavy-power, fast-action baitcasting outfit spooled with 10- to 14-pound-test mono is a good all-around choice for fishing with jigging lures. But you'll need a heavier outfit with line up to 30-pound test for fishing jigging spoons in heavy cover. In very deep water, consider using superline because the low stretch gives you a stronger hookset.

BLADEBAITS

For decades, bladebaits have been the "secret weapon" of many of the South's top smallmouth anglers, including such notables as Billy Westmorland. Using the "Silver Buddy," a bladebait with an unpainted stainless-steel body, he has taken numerous trophy-class smallmouth in mid-South reservoirs.

The intense vibrations emitted by a bladebait draw the attention of smallmouth in even the murkiest water, explaining why action is a more important consideration than color.

Some bladebaits come with a series of attachment holes on the back. Clipping your line to different holes changes the lure's action (below). Always use a Cross-Loc snap, rather than a snap-swivel, to attach the lure. Otherwise,

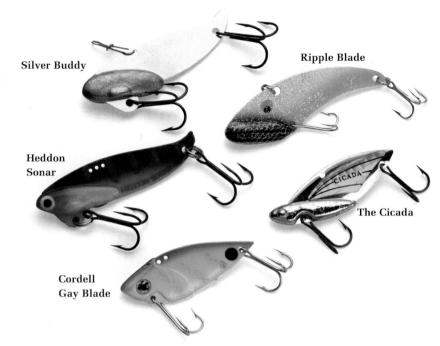

Silver Buddy

Ripple Blade

Heddon Sonar

The Cicada

Cordell Gay Blade

you'll have problems with the hooks tangling in the line.

Bladebaits are usually fished by jigging them vertically over likely structure. Because of their exposed hooks, they are not a good choice in heavy cover. On some days, the fish seem to prefer an upward sweep of several feet followed by a drop; on others, a sweep of only a foot or so works much better.

Tips for Fishing Bladebaits

Attach your clip to the middle hole (arrow) for a moderate wiggle. Attaching it to the front hole gives the lure a tighter wiggle; the rear hole, a looser wobble.

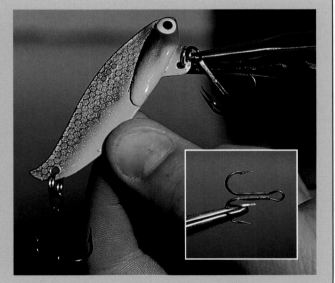

Some bladebaits come with special split-shank hooks (inset). But when these hooks get damaged, it's difficult to find replacements. If you need to change a hook, just add a split ring and an ordinary treble.

JIGGING SPOONS

Most anglers think of jigging spoons as lures for fishing deep structure, such as a cliff face, a precipitous drop-off or the base of a tree line. Because a jigging spoon is so heavy, you can fish it straight beneath your boat and place it precisely in the spot you want to fish.

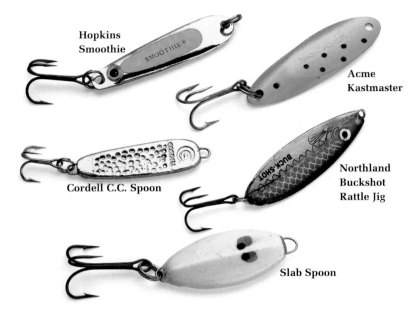

Hopkins Smoothie

Acme Kastmaster

Cordell C.C. Spoon

Northland Buckshot Rattle Jig

Slab Spoon

The weight of a jigging spoon also comes in handy for fishing woody cover. Should the lure hang up on a branch, you can often free it by lifting it and then letting it drop on a slack line.

Vertical jiggers rely mainly on long, thin jigging spoons because they sink quickly and resemble struggling baitfish. But stubby jigging spoons, called *slab spoons,* are a better choice for distance casting to smallmouth suspended in open water and feeding on shad, ciscoes or other pelagic baitfish.

Jigging spoons are one of the least expensive smallmouth lures, and many come with poor hooks and nothing but a hole in the metal for attaching your line. It's a good idea to check your hooks and replace them if necessary and add a split ring to the attachment eye so the sharp metal doesn't damage your line.

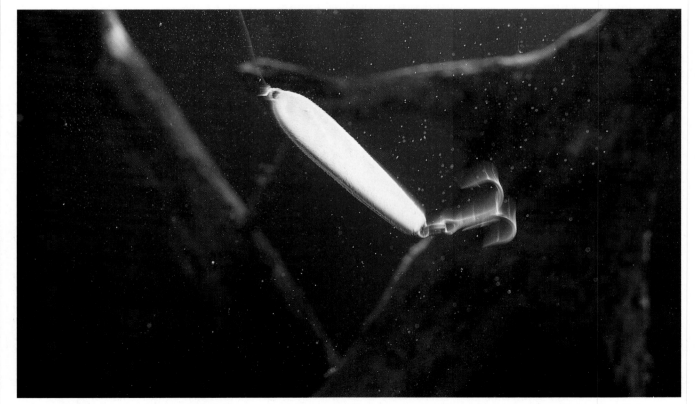

When allowed to sink on a slack line, a jigging spoon flutters out to the side, giving it a dying-baitfish action that smallmouth can't resist.

TAILSPINS

With its unique helicoptering action on the drop, a tailspin adds another dimension to vertical jigging. The spinning blade on the tail not only adds flash and vibration, it slows the sink rate, giving the fish extra time to strike.

Tailspins are also an excellent choice for casting to fish suspended in open water. With its heavy, aerodynamic body, the lure can be cast great distances, yet the helicoptering blade gives the lure enough lift that it won't sink below the level of the fish when you retrieve. If you fish a body of water where smallmouth feed on pelagic baitfish, it's a good idea to have a rod rigged with a tailspin ready to go.

You can also make a long cast, let the lure sink to the bottom and then retrieve it with a lift-and-drop motion, much as you would work a leadhead jig.

Like some jigging spoons, many tailspins often have inexpensive hooks that could result in missed strikes. Be sure to sharpen the hooks well or, if necessary, replace them with better hooks.

Flash, vibration and a slow sink rate combine to make tailspins a top smallmouth pick.

Blitz Blade

Mann's Little George

FLIES

Many smallmouth anglers take up fly fishing for the challenge and excitement of catching these powerful fighters on a bit of fur or feathers. But others get into the sport for a much more practical reason: Well-tied flies are much more convincing imitations of many important smallmouth foods than any other kind of artificial.

Besides the flies themselves, fly fishing gives you another important edge over the more popular smallmouth-fishing methods. In the hands of an accomplished flycaster,

a fly rod can get your offering into tight spots that would be virtually impossible to reach with conventional gear. Using a sidearm cast, for instance, you can easily place your fly under a limb hanging only a few inches above the water.

Although some anglers regard a fly rod as too "flimsy" for a fish that fights as hard as a smallmouth, that concern is unfounded. In fact, the extra length of a fly rod gives you more leverage for controlling the fish, and the parabolic action distributes the pressure of the fight over

the entire length of the rod, tiring the fish more quickly and acting as a cushion to reduce the chances that a sudden run will snap your line.

Smallmouth anglers generally use flies in sizes 2 to 6 and fly rods in the 6- to 8-weight range. For specifics on selecting a fly-fishing outfit, refer to page 61. Details on selecting the right fly line are discussed on page 63.

Here are some suggestions for selecting and fishing each of the commonly used fly types:

CRAYFISH FLIES

No smallmouth angler's fly box would be complete without a good selection of crayfish flies.

These sinking flies are tied on extra-long-shank hooks and have realistic-looking pincers made of hair or feathers. Most have a body wrapped with thread at intervals to represent the tail segments of a real crayfish. Some patterns are weighted to sink quickly and get down in current.

In moving water, a crayfish fly is normally fished on a dead drift, much as you would fish a streamer. At the end of the drift, however, it's a good idea to strip in line to retrieve the fly in a series of short jerks to mimic a crayfish darting along the bottom. In still water, just make a long cast, let the fly sink to the bottom and then retrieve with short strips.

Crayfish imitations form the core of the smallmouth fly angler's arsenal.

Wrap some copper or lead wire around the body of a crayfish fly if you're having trouble getting it down in the current.

Bunny Craw

Holshlag Hackle Fly

Legend Creek Crawdaddy

Legend Creek Crawdaddy

Where leeches occur, imitating them with leech flies can fool hungry bass.

LEECH FLIES

Even though leeches are not a common smallmouth food, a hungry smallmouth finds a seductively wiggling leech hard to resist. And leech flies, with their long tails made of marabou, chamois, latex or rabbit fur, have an undulating action closely resembling that of the real thing.

Many leech flies have a weighted head, with the weight commonly provided by wire windings or metal eyes. When you retrieve the fly with a jigging motion, the added weight accentuates the jigging action, giving the fly a much more leech-like appearance than a fly with no extra weight.

Leech flies range from 2 to more than 5 inches in length. If you'll be fishing in heavy cover, select a fly with a monofilament weedguard.

Lead Eyed Leech

Crystal Bugger

Electric Leech

Bunny Leech

STREAMERS

Tied on extra-long-shank hooks, streamers have an elongated shape intended to mimic shiners and other long-bodied baitfish.

There are many sub-categories of streamer flies, but the following are most popular among smallmouth anglers:

• **Hackle-Wings.** These common streamers have wings made of stiff hackle feathers that have little action in still water but flutter enticingly in current. Less buoyant than most other streamers, hackle-wings sink rapidly and are easy to get down in moving water. They are normally retrieved with a series of even strips.

• **Bucktails.** The wing, made of bucktail or other buoyant fibers, gives the fly a lifelike billowing action when retrieved with a series of even strips. Bucktails sink more slowly than hackle-wings and are used in either still water or current.

• **Marabous.** The long, fluffy marabou wing gives these flies a pulsating or "breathing" action remindful of a baitfish or larval aquatic insect working its gills.

Marabous sink slowly and should be retrieved with a twitching motion. They work well in still or moving water.

• **Jigging Flies.** Like a leech fly, a jigging fly has a weighted head or metal eyes that give the lure a seductive jigging action when fished with a twitch-and-pause retrieve. But a jigging fly has shorter wings, so it looks more like a baitfish than a leech. Like bucktails and marabous, jigging flies can be used in still water or current.

Streamers work magic on minnow-eating bronzebacks.

Clouser's Minnow (Bucktail)

Grey Ghost (Hackle Wing)

White Wooly Bugger (Jigging Fly)

EP's Bait Fish (Marabou)

Holshlag Hackle Fly

BUGS

Some of these bulky topwater flies actually do resemble "bugs," but most imitate larger morsels such as frogs and mice, and many look like nothing a fish has ever seen. Nevertheless, the surface disturbance they create quickly draws a smallmouth's attention.

Here are the types of bugs most commonly used by smallmouth fishermen:

• **Poppers.** Made of wood, cork or plastic, these hard-bodied topwaters have a flattened or cupped face that catches water and makes a distinct popping noise when you give the lure a twitch. Many poppers are dressed with hackle collars, feather tails or rubber legs.

• **Sliders.** At times, a loud popping action seems to spook smallmouth rather than attract them. If you want a topwater fly with a more subtle action, try a slider. With its bullet-shaped head, a slider skitters across the surface with minimal disturbance, and its aerodynamic shape makes it easier to cast.

• **Divers.** These flies have a seductive frog-like action, diving and making a gurgling

When fishing around woody cover, be sure to use a bug with a mono-loop weedguard.

sound when twitched sharply and then slowly floating back up on the pause. The clipped-deer-hair head and collar trap air and then emit a bubble when pulled under, accounting for the gurgling noise.

• **Hair Bugs.** These high-floating flies have a head and/or body of clipped deer or elk hair. Although many hair bugs resemble mice or frogs, their appearance really doesn't matter to the fish; all they see is a vague shape. Hair bugs are highly wind-resistant and difficult to cast, so it's a good idea to use a weight-forward or bass-bug taper fly line.

Whit's Hair Bug (Hair Bug)

Sneaky Pete (Slider)

Dahlberg Diver (Diver)

Foam Popper (Popper)

NYMPHS

These subsurface flies are realistic imitations of the immature forms of aquatic insects, such as mayfly and dragonfly nymphs.

Although most nymph patterns are sparsely dressed and not as colorful or flashy as other kinds of flies, they have tremendous fish appeal. That's because smallmouth and most other gamefish feed more heavily on the immature insect forms than on the adults. After all, the immature forms are available year-round; the adult forms, for only a few days.

Even during a heavy insect hatch, smallmouth are often feeding on the emerging nymphs rather than the adults. You might catch a few fish on a big dry fly that imitates an adult mayfly, for example, but you'd probably catch more on a mayfly nymph pattern.

Because most of the nymphs commonly eaten by smallmouth swim with an erratic darting motion, the flies are best fished with a twitch-and-pause retrieve. But don't expect a violent strike like you might get when fishing a bug. Nymphs are weak swimmers and smallmouth know it; they simply swim up to the fly and gently suck it in.

Hex Nymph

Sparrow

Theo's Terminator

Damsel Nymph

Murry's Hellgrammite

Smallmouth cruise about lazily during an insect hatch, inhaling immature insects as they struggle toward the surface. Whenever you feel a slight nudge or just a little resistance, set the hook.

FISHING WITH LIVE BAIT

When the "bite" is on, you'll seldom need live bait to catch smallmouth. But when the going gets tough, a lively crawler, leech, crayfish or minnow can save the day.

Live bait works especially well in clear water, where smallmouth can closely inspect your offering. But the scent of live bait draws smallmouth in discolored water too.

Live bait also excels when frigid water temperatures slow smallmouth feeding activity. At water temperatures below 50°F, a lively bait is almost always more effective than an artificial.

The major downside to live bait is that it must be fished slowly. This means you can't cover nearly as much water as you can with a crankbait or other fast-moving lure. Many smallmouth anglers rely on artificials to locate aggressive biters, and then switch to live bait when the action slows.

For the most realistic presentation, most smallmouth experts fish live bait on a plain slip-sinker, slip-bobber or split-shot rig, with no spinners, beads or other attractors. But live bait is also commonly used for tipping artificials such as jigs, spinners, spinnerbaits and even flies.

Besides crawlers, leeches and minnows, which are available at most bait shops, smallmouth anglers rely on

some unusual baits including frogs, salamanders, hellgrammites (dobson-fly larvae), grasshoppers and crickets. These baits are more difficult to find and may even be illegal to sell, so you'll probably have to collect them yourself.

Here are some guidelines on when, where and how to use each of these live baits:

NIGHTCRAWLERS

A lively crawler ranks high on the list of the top smallmouth baits. Crawlers are widely available at bait shops and it's easy to collect or even raise your own. And they're among the easiest baits to keep for extended periods. Just go out to your local golf course and pick up a mess of worms on a rainy spring night, put them in some worm bedding and keep them in a cool place—you'll have worms well into the fall.

Crawlers work well in most any kind of still or moving water, but they're mainly a warmwater bait. Although there are exceptions, they generally work best at water temperatures of 60°F or higher.

The size of your crawler can make a big difference in your smallmouth-fishing success. Huge "rattlesnakes"—those foot-long crawlers often used by walleye fishermen—are not a good choice for smallmouth. The fish don't hesitate to take them, but you'll be lucky to hook one fish for every three pick-ups. Your hooking percentage will improve considerably if you select a 6- or 7-inch worm.

The condition of your crawlers is also a major concern. If you let them warm up too much, they'll get mushy and won't react to a touch. What you want is a firm-bodied crawler that squirms wildly when a smallmouth grabs it.

Crawlers offer one big advantage over other kinds of live bait. They can be inflated with a "worm blower" or a syringe to make them float off the bottom; this way, your hook is less likely to hang up or catch bottom-hugging weeds or algae.

The main problem with using crawlers: They're not only a favorite of smallmouth, they attract many other kinds of fish as well. If you're fishing in a body of water infested with small perch or sunfish, for example, they'll quickly nip the end off your worm, making it much less effective for smallmouth.

> ## Effective Crawler-Rigging Methods*
>
> - Slip-sinker rig with plain short-shank hook or floater.
> - Split-shot rig and plain hook.
> - Slip-bobber rig with plain short-shank hook or 1/16-ounce jig head.
> - Spin-rig or small spinnerbait tipped with piece of crawler.
> - Piece of crawler on a French or Sonic spinner.
> - Jig head tipped with small crawler or half of a large one.
> - Bit of crawler on subsurface fly.
>
> *Refer to pages 134-137 for rigging details.

How to Hook a Crawler

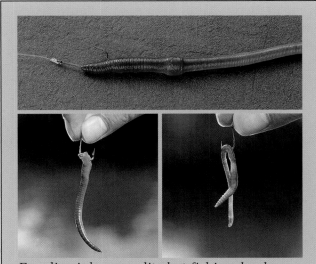

For slip-sinker or split-shot fishing, hook a crawler through the head so it trails straight (top). For tipping a jig or spinner, use half a crawler hooked through the broken end (bottom left). For float fishing, hook it through the middle (bottom right).

How to Inflate a Crawler

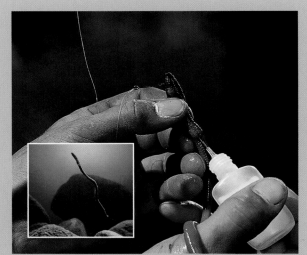

Using a worm blower or hypodermic needle, squeeze a small bubble of air into the worm's collar. This way, the worm will float level and have a lifelike look. If you squeeze air into the worm's tail, the worm will trail with its tail up and look unnatural (inset).

LEECHES

Strange thing about leeches and smallmouth: The fish pay little attention to the leech species most commonly found in smallmouth waters, but they love ribbon leeches, which are inhabitants of small ponds and marshes that have never seen a smallmouth.

Ribbon leeches have been a favorite of northern small-mouth anglers for years, and their popularity is spreading as they are exported to bait dealers in other parts of the country. If you can't find ribbon leeches at your local bait shop, you can probably catch smallmouth on other kinds of leeches, but you may have to trap your own and do some experimenting to see if the fish like them.

The enticing wiggle of a lively leech quickly gets the attention of smallmouth, even when the bite is off. Savvy anglers know that a leech presented very slowly, either on a split-shot rig or slip-bobber rig, is one of the very best cold-front techniques.

Like nightcrawlers, leeches are most popular in warm weather. At water tempera-

Make sure your leech maintains its flattened shape and swims continuously. If it barely swims at all and its body becomes round (inset), discard it.

tures below 50°F, a leech often curls up into a tight ball and refuses to swim.

Leeches are a better choice than crawlers in waters with lots of panfish. A perch or sunfish can nip off the end of a crawler in a heartbeat; it takes a lot more chewing to bite off a leech. But even a leech can't stand up to constant pummeling by panfish. Once your leech stops swimming and loses its flattened shape, put on a fresh one.

You can keep leeches for months without feeding them, but they must be refrigerated in clean, dechlorinated water. Once they are allowed to warm up, the larger ones begin to spawn and will soon die.

It doesn't take huge leeches to catch smallmouth. You'll get just as many bites on a 2½- to 4-inch leech as you will on a 6-inch "mud flap," and you'll miss far fewer fish.

How to Hook Leeches

For most smallmouth fishing, hook your leech just ahead of the sucker (left). When nibbling panfish are a problem, hook it through the tough skin of the neck (middle). When float fishing, hook it through the middle (right).

Effective Leech-Rigging Methods*

- Slip-sinker rig with plain short-shank hook or floater.
- Split-shot rig and plain hook.
- Slip-bobber rig with plain short-shank hook or ¹⁄₁₆-ounce jig head.
- Spin-rig or small spinnerbait tipped with small leech.
- Small leech on a French or Sonic spinner.
- Jig head tipped with small leech.

*Refer to pages 134-137 for rigging details.

CRAYFISH

In waters where crayfish abound, they often make up the majority of a smallmouth's diet. So it's easy to understand why they make awesome smallmouth bait.

But despite their effectiveness, crayfish are not as popular among smallmouth anglers as they once were. Concerns over introducing harmful species, such as the rusty crayfish, have led to laws prohibiting the sale of crayfish for bait in many states. Be sure to check your state's regulations before fishing with crayfish; it may be legal to catch your own and use them for bait, but they should not be transported to other waters.

There are more than 500 species of crayfish in North America, but species is not as important as size. A 2½- to 3½-incher is ideal for smallmouth. They'll grab bigger ones, but may not take them deeply enough for you to get a good hookset.

Although many anglers swear by "softshell" craws, those that have just recently molted, hardshells will catch

When a smallmouth grabs your craw, don't set the hook right away. It may take up to 30 seconds for the fish to take the craw deeply enough for a good hookset. The bigger the craw, the longer you should wait before setting.

plenty of smallmouth as well. Some fishermen tear off the claws to give the craw a smaller profile and make it look less "forbidding."

You can collect crayfish simply by turning over flat rocks in a stream or along a lakeshore and catching them with a dip net as they scurry away. If you want to keep them alive for an extended period, put them in a cooler with just enough water to keep their gills moist. Keep

them refrigerated and change the water every few days.

Effective Crayfish-Rigging Methods*

- Slip-sinker rig with plain or weedless hook.
- Split-shot rig with plain or weedless hook.

*Refer to pages 134–137 for rigging details.

How to Hook Crayfish

Through Snout. *If your crayfish has a large, tough "horn" on its head, push a single hook through the horn as shown. This way, the craw is less likely to scoot backwards and get under a rock.*

Through Tail. *If the horn is too small or fragile, push the hook through the side of the next to last segment of the tail.*

BAITFISH

If you could only use one smallmouth bait year-round, the best choice—hands down—would be baitfish. Unlike most other kinds of live bait, they'll catch smallmouth at any water temperature and they're available every month of the year.

Most smallmouth fishermen prefer baitfish from 3 to 4 inches long. In fall, however, when the natural forage crop has increased in size, 5- or even 6-inchers sometimes work better.

Smallmouth feed on hundreds of different kinds of baitfish, any of which would make decent fishing bait. But most anglers are limited by what they can buy at their local bait shop. Here are the kinds of baitfish most popular among smallmouth anglers:

Shiners

Although shiners are one of the least hardy types of baitfish, there is no better smallmouth bait. They work best during coolwater periods and may be difficult to keep alive at water temperatures above 60°F.

More than 100 kinds of shiners are found in North American waters, with many different species being popular in different regions. In most cases, however, slim-bodied types such as emerald and spottail shiners are more popular than deep-bodied species like common or red shiners.

Chubs

Much hardier than shiners, chubs are a favorite of river fishermen, but they also work well in lakes and reservoirs. Dozens of kinds of chubs are found in smallmouth waters,

and anglers have their local favorites. In the north-central states, for example, horny-head (redtail) chubs are the top choice of many fishermen. Although they're expensive and may be difficult to find, their reddish fins and great endurance make them an exceptional bait.

If you can't find chubs at your local bait shop, you can probably catch your own by fishing in a small stream, using a bit of worm for bait.

Fathead Minnows

Technically, fatheads are a type of chub, but they're even hardier than most other chub species. Sometimes called "tuffies" or "mudminnows," these common baitfish do not have the smallmouth appeal of a shiner or redtail, but they're easier to keep alive in warm weather. In spring, the males turn black and develop breeding tubercles on their head while the females remain silvery. The females make much better bait.

Dace

If you pull a minnow seine through a rocky stream in practically any part of the country, you're likely to haul in a mess of dace.

Among the most common dace species and a favorite of smallmouth anglers is the colorful red-belly dace. In many bait shops, they're sold as "rainbows."

Dace are quite hardy and, if you keep them well aerated,

will stay alive even in warm water.

Shad

Shad are among the most delicate of all baitfish, so you won't find live ones at a bait shop. But these silvery, soft-bodied baitfish are a major smallmouth food in many rivers and reservoirs, particularly in the South, and knowledgeable anglers have learned to collect their own using cast nets and dip nets.

Serious fishermen keep their shad in large, insulated, aerated tanks. If you keep them in your boat's live well or an ordinary minnow bucket, they'll die almost immediately.

Smallmouth feed on both gizzard and threadfin shad, but gizzards are hardier and make better bait.

Oddities

Anglers in certain regions use a number of unusual baitfish that have exceptional smallmouth appeal.

Along the Mississippi River, for example, veteran anglers know that no other bait works as well for smallmouth as a lively madtom, or "willow cat," which is a tiny member of the catfish family. And some West-Coast fishermen swear by small American eels, called "pencil eels."

Effective Minnow-Rigging Methods*

- Slip-bobber rig with plain hook or small jig.
- Slip-sinker rig with plain hook or floater.
- Split-shot rig.
- Jig and minnow.
- Jigging spoon with whole minnow or minnow head.
- Spin-rig and minnow.

*Refer to pages 134–137 for rigging details.

Baitfish for Smallmouth

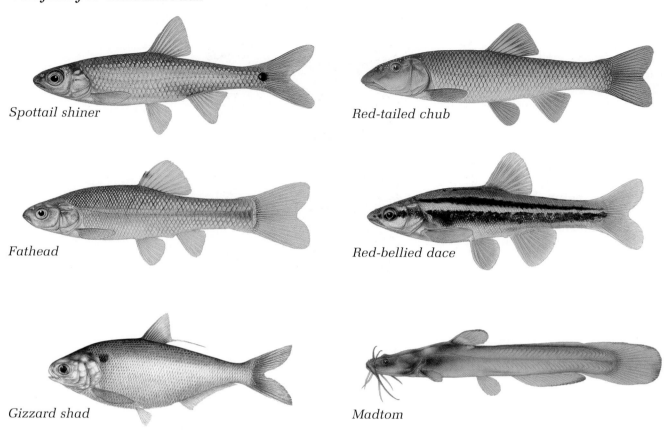

Spottail shiner

Red-tailed chub

Fathead

Red-bellied dace

Gizzard shad

Madtom

How to Hook Baitfish

When retrieving baitfish, hook them (1) through the lips or (2) through the mouth and out the top of the head. For still-fishing, hook them (3) below the dorsal fin or (4) through the tail. Shad stay on the hook better if you hook them (5) through the nostrils.

SPRING LIZARDS

In waters of the southeastern U.S., spring lizards have long been a top smallmouth producer. Some anglers will tell you that smallmouth attack lizards because they pose a threat to their nests, but that doesn't explain why smallmouth hit lizards long after the spawning period as well.

Spring lizards are adult salamanders belonging to a group called "lungless" salamanders. These sleek-bodied amphibians are smaller than most other salamanders and they're good swimmers, explaining why they work so well for bait.

You can buy spring lizards at bait shops and roadside stands in parts of the Southeast, but they're not always available when you want them. To collect your own, walk along a spring or brook after dark with a flashlight and dip net. Or, look for lizards in window wells after a rainy night. You can keep them alive for weeks in a container filled with damp moss and kept in a cool spot.

Fishing with spring lizards presents some special prob-

To catch short strikers, use a short length of mono to attach a size 8 or 10 treble hook to the bend of your main hook. Push the "stinger" into the body behind the hind leg.

lems: If you hook a lizard through the lips, it may squirm its way off the hook and escape. But you can secure it with small plastic tabs punched from the lid of a coffee can (below).

If you use a lizard more than 5 inches long, you'll get a lot of short strikes and miss too many fish. If you don't have smaller bait, you can catch the short strikers by tying on a stinger hook (above).

> ## Effective Salamander-Rigging Methods*
>
> • Slip-sinker rig with plain or weedless hook.
> • Split-shot rig with plain or weedless hook.
> • Small spring lizard on plain or weedless jig head.
>
> *Refer to pages 134-137 for rigging details.

How to Hook Spring Lizards

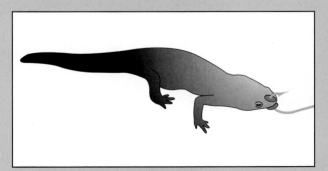

Push a plastic tab onto your hook bend, push the hook through the lips and then add another tab. This way, the lizard cannot squirm free of the hook.

Hook a lizard through the tough skin just ahead of the hind leg. The lizard cannot free itself from the hook and it will stay alive longer than it would if hooked through the lips.

WATERDOGS

At about 6 inches in length, the average waterdog is a bit too large for the majority of smallmouth fishing. But if you're fishing on waters known for trophies, a good-sized waterdog is one of the very best baits.

A waterdog is the larval aquatic form of the tiger salamander, many species of which are found throughout the U.S. and southern Canada. Waterdogs are easy to identify because of their external gills, tiny legs and long fin that runs completely around the rear half of the body.

When buying waterdogs, make sure you're getting the larval form. If the waterdogs have started to transform into adults, which have no gills or tail fin and sport the characteristic black and yellow coloration, they're much less effective as bait. Instead of swimming seductively, they lie motionless on the bottom or crawl along slowly.

If you can't find waterdogs at a bait shop, it's fairly easy to collect your own by seining shallow ponds before they dry up in late summer. If you have a lot of waterdogs to choose from, select the smaller ones, preferably 4- to 5-inchers. You can keep them alive for months in a container of clean water at a temperature of about 50°F.

Waterdogs are rigged and fished pretty much the same way as spring lizards, and fishing with them presents

A big waterdog is a top trophy smallmouth bait.

the same problems. They're difficult to keep on the hook, so you may have to use plastic tabs, and the fish tend to strike short, making a stinger hook a good option.

Waterdog vs. Adult Tiger Salamander

Waterdog. *The background color is a uniform brown or olive and the gills are very distinct. A long fin wraps around the rear of the body and the legs are much smaller than those of an adult tiger salamander.*

Adult Tiger Salamander. *The coloration varies greatly among species, but most have some sort of black-and-yellow barred or spotted pattern. The gills and tail fin have disappeared, and the legs are well developed.*

FROGS

Kids that fish for stream smallmouth rarely stop at the bait shop before hitting the water. They bring a rod and reel, a few extra hooks and sinkers and a container to carry the frogs and crayfish they catch along the stream.

While most anglers think of frogs as a superb bait for largemouth, they work just as well for smallmouth. Frogs are most effective during their migration in fall, when smallmouth feed on frogs moving from shallow ponds, where they spent the summer, to deeper bodies of water, where they will winter.

Frogs around 3 inches long make the best smallmouth bait. The fish will hit larger frogs, but you'll have trouble setting the hook. Although leopard frogs are the species most commonly used as bait, green frogs and other small frogs will also work.

If you're quick, you can catch all the frogs you need by hand. But a dip net makes the job a lot easier. If you'll be collecting a lot of frogs, keep them in a screen box with a slitted-rubber top that lets you grab one without the others escaping.

A frog works best when weighted lightly so it can swim freely.

Effective Frog-Rigging Methods*

- Slip-sinker rig with plain or weedless hook.
- Split-shot rig with plain or weedless hook.
- Freelining or dabbling with plain hook and no extra weight.

Refer to pages 134-137 for rigging details.

How to Hook a Frog

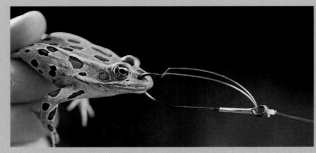

For the majority of your fishing, hook a frog through the lips using a plain or weedless hook. If you'll be doing a lot of casting, secure the frog with plastic tabs (p. 130).

For freelining, hook a frog through the hind leg. This method also works well for float fishing.

INSECTS

No discussion of "on-site" smallmouth baits is complete without mentioning insects. Besides the obvious adult forms like grasshoppers and crickets, some of the larval forms make excellent bait as well. In fact, many stream-fishing authorities consider hellgrammites (dobson-fly larvae), the very best stream-smallmouth bait. Dragonfly nymphs also work well.

Hoppers and crickets are a good choice on a warm summer day, when the fish are slurping drifting insects off the surface. You can catch the insects by hand or with a dip net and keep them in a cricket container that dispenses them one at a time.

Larval insects work best in summer and fall. The best way to catch them is to hold a fine mesh net downstream of a rocky area in a stream while your partner turns over rocks to dislodge them. To keep them alive, put them in a Styrofoam minnow bucket and keep it cool and well aerated.

When hoppers are active streamside, they also make great smallmouth bait.

Effective Insect-Rigging Methods*

Adult Forms:
• Split-shot rig and extra-long-shank hook.
• Insect floated on surface with extra-long-shank hook (no extra weight).

Larval Forms:
• Split-shot rig and plain hook.
• Fixed- or slip-bobber rig with split-shot and plain hook.

*Refer to pages 134-137 for rigging details.

Thread a hopper or cricket onto a light-wire, extra-long-shank hook either (1) head-first or (2) tail-first. Hook a (3) hellgrammite or (4) dragonfly nymph under the collar using a light-wire hook.

LIVE-BAIT PRESENTATIONS

There are days when small-mouth will eagerly attack practically any kind of live bait on any kind of rig. But those times are rare; more often, it takes just the right presentation to entice the fish to bite.

The main things to consider when trying to determine the best presentation are water depth, type of cover and the mood of the fish. Fail to take any of these factors into account and you'll have little chance of success.

This means you'll have to become proficient with a variety of presentations, with the following of greatest importance:

SLIP-SINKER FISHING

With a slip-sinker rig, a smallmouth can pick up your bait and move off without feeling resistance. This way, the fish is much less likely to drop the bait than if it were

towing a sinker affixed to the line.

Most slip-sinker fishing involves slow trolling with an open-face spinning outfit. This way, you can keep the bail open and then release the line when you feel a tug. You can also cast and retrieve a slip-sinker rig, but you must be quick to drop back your rod tip or open the bail when you detect a bite.

Rods used for slip-sinker fishing should have a relatively soft tip so the fish doesn't feel too much resistance and drop the bait. After hesitating for a few seconds to let the fish run, quickly reel up the slack until you feel weight and then set the hook.

The basic slip-sinker rig (right) includes an egg sinker and a short-shank bait hook, but there are many variations intended for specific purposes. In weedy cover, for example, you may want to substitute a bullet sinker (p. 143) for the egg sinker. And on a rocky bottom, a snag-resistant sinker and possibly a floater will minimize hang-ups.

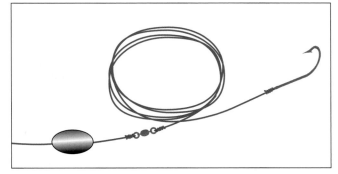

To make a basic slip-sinker rig, thread an egg or walking sinker onto your line, tie in a small barrel swivel as a stop and then add a 3- to 4-foot leader and the appropriate bait hook.

Tips for Slip-Sinker Fishing

Substitute a slip-bobber knot and bead for a barrel swivel. Then you can easily adjust your leader length by moving the knot up or down the line.

Use a rod with a soft tip but a stiff butt. This way, the fish won't feel much resistance when it picks up the bait, but you'll still get a strong hookset.

When a smallmouth picks up your bait and runs off, it often puts a bow or loop in your line. If you don't reel up all the slack before setting the hook, you'll just pull in the loose line and never reach the fish.

SPLIT-SHOTTING

Shallow-water smallmouth are extra spooky and won't put up with bombardment by a heavily-weighted bait rig. But they don't seem to mind the gentle entry of a rig weighted with only a split-shot.

Split-shotting has other advantages as well. With the rig weighted so lightly, you're forced to retrieve very slowly in order to keep your bait close to the bottom. And when a fish picks up the bait, it feels very little resistance. Another big plus: Should you get snagged and lose your rig, it takes just a few seconds to tie on another hook and pinch on a shot.

To achieve a super-slow presentation and detect even the lightest take, some anglers use a technique called "stitching," picking up a few inches of line at a time with their fingers (below). The method works especially well with baits like crayfish and spring lizards, because they must be

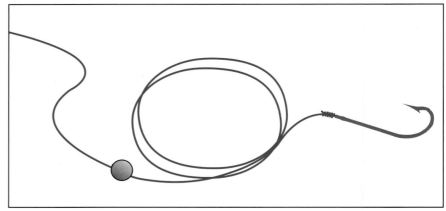

Tie on the appropriate bait hook and then pinch on a split-shot from 12 to 18 inches up the line.

crawled very slowly along the bottom to be effective.

Split-shotting works well in either still or moving water, but it's especially valuable in stream fishing because you can angle your cast upstream and let the bait drift naturally with the current while barely bumping the bottom. The key to success with this method, however, is selecting shot of exactly the right size. Too heavy and you'll hang up

constantly; too light and your bait won't get to the bottom.

In still, shallow water, you may want to eliminate the split-shot altogether and "freeline" the bait. This is the most natural of all live-bait presentations.

As in slip-sinker fishing, it's important to use a rod with a soft tip. Not only will it prevent the fish from feeling resistance, it makes casting the light rig much easier.

The Stitching Technique (Right-Handed Angler, Spinning Outfit)

1 Stitch in line by first grabbing it with the thumb and forefinger of your left hand.

2 Next, double up the line and catch it with your other fingers.

3 Then grab the line again with your thumb and forefinger, at the same time dropping the loop you just picked up.

SLIP-BOBBER FISHING

The idea of sitting around and watching a bobber may not appeal to some anglers, but there are times when slip-bobber fishing will outproduce any other method.

When smallmouth are suspended in open water, for example, they often hold in a narrow layer, making it difficult to keep your bait at their level. But with a slip-bobber rig, you can set your float to keep your bait right in the fish zone.

Under cold-front conditions or whenever the fish are in a negative feeding mood, they're not likely to chase a moving bait. But you may be able to tempt a few bites by using a slip-bobber setup to dangle the bait right in their face.

You don't necessarily need a slip-bobber rig for fishing in water only a few feet deep, but a slip-bobber rig is much easier to cast than a fixed-bobber rig with several feet of line dangling beneath the float.

In setting up your slip-bobber rig, it's important to add just the right amount of weight. If you don't add enough, the float will ride too high and the fish will feel too much resistance when it takes the bait. If you add too much, your bait may pull the float under or it may dip under from wave action, mimicking a bite.

With most baits, it's a good idea to set the hook as soon as the float goes down; otherwise, the fish may feel resistance and let go. Because of the sharp angle that forms between you and your bait (below), it may be difficult to get a firm hookset. When you detect a bite, rapidly reel up slack until you feel the fish's weight and then set the hook with a quick snap of the wrists.

Serious slip-bobber fishermen use a longer-than-normal spinning rod (7 to 7½ feet) because it takes up more slack on the hookset and has better hook-setting leverage. A high-speed spinning reel also helps take up slack more quickly.

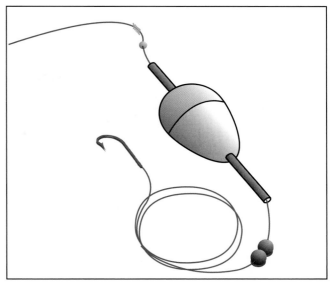

Tie a slip-bobber knot on your line, then thread on a small bead and the bobber. Finish the rig by tying on the appropriate hook and adding split-shot about a foot up the line.

Slip-Bobber Tips

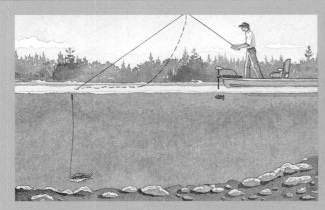

A slip-bobber rig puts a sharp angle between you and the fish, so it may be difficult to get a solid hookset. To solve the problem, reel up to remove all the slack (dotted line) before setting.

When tying a slip-bobber knot, don't trim the tag ends. If you do, the stiff ends of the knot will protrude from your reel's spool and prevent line from flowing off smoothly when you cast.

BEYOND THE BASICS

*T*op small-mouth pros have a bag of tricks that help them catch small-mouth in every imaginable situation. Here's how they do it.

FISHING IN WEEDY COVER

Smallmouth are much less weed-oriented than large-mouth, but there are many situations in which they're drawn to weedy cover.

In a lake with a rocky basin and very little weedy cover, for example, smallmouth often relate to what few weed patches there are. But in a weedy lake, smallmouth are more likely to hang around rocky areas. It's almost as if they prefer something different from the predominant cover type.

Unlike largemouth, small-mouth are seldom found in dense weeds. They prefer sparse vegetation where they can easily maneuver to catch baitfish or other prey. While a largemouth may hang out in the middle of a thick weed bed or under a dense mat of weeds, a smallmouth is more likely to lurk along the edge of the weeds, darting out into the open to grab food.

Another major difference: Largemouth can be found in weeds growing on a soft or hard bottom, but smallmouth definitely prefer vegetation on a firm sandy, gravelly or rocky bottom. This means you'll rarely find smallmouth in lily pads, cattails or other weeds associated with a muddy or silty substrate.

Smallmouth usually favor weedbeds near deep water. For instance, a weedy hump or point that drops rapidly into water at least 25 feet deep is much more likely to hold smallmouth than a weedy flat of uniform depth with no deep water nearby.

Fishing in weedy cover requires heavier-than-normal spinning or baitcasting gear and 10- to 17-pound-test, abrasion-resistant line. If you go lighter, you won't be able to turn a fish heading for dense weeds and, if the line wraps around the stems, you won't have enough power to pull it free.

If you're like a lot of other smallmouth anglers, you avoid weedy cover because you don't like the hassle of constantly picking weeds off your hook. But you can fish practically any kind of weedy cover with a minimum of fouling. Here's how:

Bulrushes. North America has more than 50 species of bulrushes, also called "reeds" or "pencil reeds." These emergent plants have round, leafless stems that range in color from light green to dark green. They taper to a sharp point on top and may have a brownish flower at the tip. The best bulrushes grow in deep water (5 feet or more).

SUBMERGENT WEEDS

Submergent vegetation will hold smallmouth from the time it first appears in spring to the time it dies back in fall. But remember that not all the weeds in a given lake die at the same time. If you look around, you should be able to find clumps of green weeds well into the fall or even the winter. And the green weeds will invariably draw more smallmouth than the brown, dead ones.

Any underwater plant that provides shade and hiding cover has smallmouth potential. But for reasons that only the smallmouth know, they're drawn to some kinds of submergent weeds more than others. Here are a few of their favorites, along with some tips for fishing them:

EMERGENT WEEDS

Emergents that grow on a firm bottom, such as bulrushes, are springtime smallmouth favorites. And if the plants are adjacent to deep water, they may also hold smallmouth in summer and early fall.

Most emergent plants have few if any leaves to catch your bait, so fouling is not as much of a problem as it would be if fishing in leafy vegetation. This means you can use a variety of lures including topwaters, spinnerbaits, jigs and soft plastics. These lures can easily be threaded through narrow slots in the vegetation without constantly hanging up. But it's a good idea to stay away from stickbaits or other lures with a wide lateral action because they'll scoot sideways and tangle around the weed stems.

Cabbage

The term "cabbage" refers to several types of pondweed that have crispy, cabbage-like leaves. As a rule, the broadleaf varieties are more

Good Cabbage vs. Poor Cabbage

Broad-leaved types of cabbage, such as Richardson's pondweed (left) provide better cover than narrow-leaved types, such as curled pondweed (right). Broadleaf cabbage may grow in water as deep as 14 feet.

appealing to smallmouth than the narrow-leaf types (p. 141). In most cases, cabbage beds with loosely spaced plants will hold more than those that grow in a dense cluster or mat.

Because cabbage has crispy leaves that shatter easily, you can run a crankbait or other open-hooked lure along the weedline or even through a sparse stand with few problems. If you do hook some weeds, a sharp snap of the rod will usually solve the problem.

Besides crankbaits, minnowbaits and rattlebaits, other good choices for fishing cabbage include spinnerbaits, jig worms, Texas- or Carolina-rigged worms and grubs, and live bait on a bullet-sinker rig. The best cabbage beds are more than 10 feet deep, so the fish may be reluctant to rise for a topwater. Those are the cases in which you'll need to "get down" to the bass.

Coontail

As its name suggests, this plant has the bushy shape of a raccoon's tail. It grows in dense clusters, usually on a firm bottom, and is sometimes found at depths exceeding 30 feet.

Coontail has tough stems that will not easily break or shatter, so it's difficult to pull an open-hooked lure through a coontail bed. This means you'll have to work the edges or else use a weedless lure or bait rig. Top picks include jig worms, Texas- or Carolina-rigged worms and grubs, slow-rolled spinnerbaits and live bait on a bullet-sinker rig. Coontail beds are generally too deep for topwaters.

Milfoil

At first glance, you could easily mistake milfoil for coontail, but the two plants really have little in common. Milfoil does not grow as deep

as coontail and does not form dense mats on the bottom. Instead, the individual plants grow vertically and may mat out to form a canopy on the surface. Underneath the canopy, the fish can maneuver easily through the vertical stems.

Another difference: Milfoil does not necessarily grow on a firm bottom, although that's where you'll normally find the most smallmouth.

Milfoil is not as tough as coontail, meaning that you can normally remove fouled weeds with a sharp jerk of the rod. This opens the door for using lures with exposed hooks like crankbaits, minnowbaits, rattlebaits, jig worms and Carolina-rigged worms and grubs. You can also work the fringes using an open-hook live-bait rig with a bullet sinker. Spinnerbaits, brush-guard jigs and Texas-rigged soft plastics round out the list of popular milfoil lures.

How to Recognize Coontail and Milfoil

Coontail. *One of the most common types of deepwater vegetation, coontail may grow to a depth of 35 feet in clearwater lakes. It usually grows on a firm bottom in dense masses up to 10 feet thick. The plants are not rooted. Coontail resembles milfoil but the stems are green and the individual leaflets (inset) are not branched.*

Milfoil. *There are 13 species of milfoil in North America, including Eurasian water milfoil, an unwelcome exotic that crowds out other native aquatic plants but makes good fish cover. Milfoil differs from coontail in that the plants are rooted, the stems are usually pinkish or reddish and the individual leaflets (inset) are branched.*

How To Catch Smallmouth Bass

Tips for Fishing in Weedy Cover

This angler is fishing bulrushes the wrong way: with the wind at his back. Rather, you should cast into a bulrush bed with the wind in your face. This way, the plants are bending toward you so your lure is much less likely to catch on the stems.

Rip a crankbait through a sparse cabbage bed to trigger smallmouth strikes. If you hang up, a sharp jerk will shatter the crispy leaves.

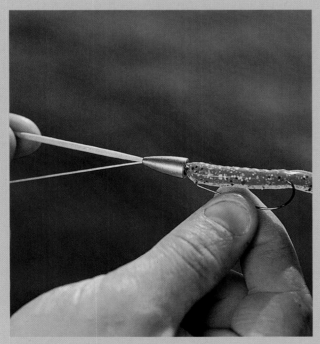

Texas-rig a worm, lizard, grub or craw to fish stringy weeds that won't shatter. To prevent the bullet sinker from separating from the lure and causing hang-ups, peg it onto the line with a piece of toothpick.

Use a bullet-sinker rig with a weedless hook to fish live bait in weedy cover. If you're missing too many fish, the weedguard may be too stiff. Loosen it up by trimming off a few of the wire bristles.

FISHING IN WOODY COVER

To a novice smallmouth angler, a tangle of woody cover looks like a good place to lose lures—and fish. But smallmouth pros know that woody cover makes prime bronzeback habitat. Not only does it provide shade and ambush cover, it harbors insects and other invertebrates that attract baitfish, giving smallmouth an inexhaustible supply of food.

Practically any kind of woody cover—including standing timber, fallen trees, logs, stumps and brush piles—can hold smallmouth. But newly submerged trees and brush, with most of their small branches still intact, attract the most fish. Once the branches rot away, the cover provides less food.

The best woody cover is usually close to deep water. A stump, log or brush pile far up on a shallow flat will seldom hold many fish.

Catching smallmouth in woody cover requires some special casting methods. Not only must you place your cast precisely to fish tight pockets in the cover, you must cast with a low trajectory to get your lure under branches and ensure a gentle entry into the water.

For close-range targets, you can swing your lure into the fish zone with a method called *flippin'*. Using a 7½-foot, heavy-power, fast-action flippin' stick combined with a baitcasting reel spooled with 20- to 30-pound mono, you can strip off line and drop a weedless jig or Texas-rigged soft plastic into the tightest spot.

To reach targets at longer range, try *pitchin'*. Instead of stripping off line and swinging your jig or soft plastic toward the target, you cast it with an upward sweep of the rod. Pitchin' is usually done with a 6½-foot, medium-heavy-power, fast-action rod paired with a narrow-spool baitcasting reel filled with 14- to 20-pound mono. A wider spool may have too much momentum, causing frequent backlashes.

When you feel a take in woody cover, set the hook hard and immediately horse the fish out of the tangle. If you don't, it will invariably wrap you around a branch.

It's almost impossible to fish woody cover without learning to flip and pitch, but these methods also come in handy for fishing pockets in the weeds, getting under overhanging obstacles or fishing in any shallow-water situation that demands a silent lure entry.

Flippin'. *Pull out as much line as you think you'll need to reach your target. Let a rod's length of line dangle from the rod tip and hold the excess line in your other hand (left). With your rod pointed upward and in the direction of your target, swing the lure toward your body and then propel the lure toward your target with a smooth, level motion of the rod tip (right). Be sure to keep the trajectory as low as possible so the lure does not splash down too hard.*

Pitchin'. *Strip off enough line that you can cradle the lure in the palm of your hand; the head of the lure should be pointing in the direction you want to cast (inset, left). With your reel in free-spool and the spool tension loose, hold your reel at chest level and point your rod tip slightly downward (left). Sweep the rod forward and slightly upward to pull the lure out of your hand and propel it toward your target on a low trajectory (right). Raising the rod too high elevates the trajectory. Thumb the reel to stop the lure so it settles down softly in the precise spot.*

FISHING ROCKY COVER

If you spend a lot of time fishing in rocky cover, you know that small boulders or broken chunks of rock are more likely to attract smallmouth than large, flat "slab" rocks. But when you're fishing boulders or chunk rock, snags are inevitable. Here are some tips for keeping hang-ups to a minimum:

• **Stay vertical.** When fishing with live bait on a slip-sinker rig, your sinker will frequently wedge between the rocks, and you may lose your entire rig. But you can minimize the number of hang-ups by using a heavier-than-normal sinker and keeping your line as close to vertical as possible.

• **Use a snag-resistant sinker.** Although no sinker is completely snag-proof, some are more snag-resistant than others. Some anglers swear by flexible sinkers made by filling up a piece of parachute cord with lead shot. Others prefer commercially made models, such as the Lindy No-Snagg sinker.

• **Add a floater.** Adding a float to your line or using a floating jig head will keep your hook above the rocks. When using a floater, be sure to move your rig very slowly; otherwise, your bait won't float up.

• **Use a long rod.** With a longer-than-normal rod, you can pull on a snag from a variety of angles without moving your boat, increasing the chances of dislodging the snagged hook or sinker. Some anglers who fish rocky lakes use rods up to 8½ feet in length.

• **Try bobber fishing.** If you're still getting snagged after trying all these methods, attach a slip-bobber to keep your bait a few inches off the bottom.

• **Carry a plug knocker.** You can buy a variety of "plug knockers" designed to slide down your line to dislodge snagged lures. In shallow water, you can poke your lure free using a long pole with a wire pigtail on the end.

Your choice of line is also important when fishing rocky cover. Sharp-edged rocks will abrade any line and may even cut off superline. The best all-around line for rocky cover is a hard-finish mono.

The Importance of Staying Vertical

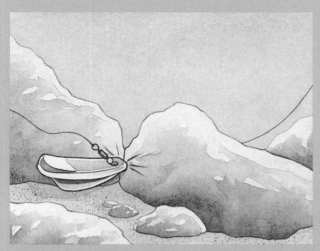
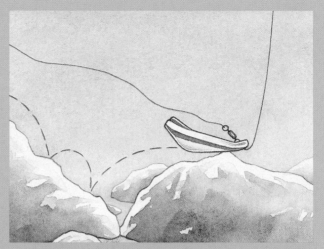

When you let your line drag (left), your angle of pull is very low, so the odds of your sinker wedging between rocks are high. But with your line near vertical (right), your sinker will pull up and over most of the rocks, rather than wedge between them.

Rigs for Fishing Rocky Cover

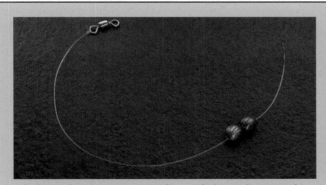
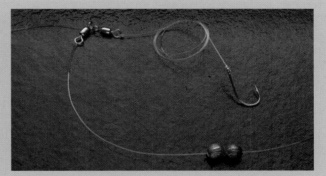

Sliding dropper rig. Make a sliding dropper by tying a barrel swivel to one end of a foot-long piece of mono and pinching split-shot onto the other (left). Then, thread the barrel swivel onto your line in place of a slip-sinker (right). The split-shot may wedge in the rocks but a strong tug will pull them off the dropper, freeing the rest of the rig.

Jig head and bait. Use a plain jig head tipped with live bait in place of a slip-sinker rig. The hook point on a jig head rides up, keeping snags to a minimum, and even if you do get snagged, retying takes only a few seconds.

Blown-up crawler. When fishing with nightcrawlers, use a worm blower to inject a little air into the collar to lift the bait above the rocks.

FISHING CLEAR WATER

Clear water is a mixed blessing for smallmouth anglers. When smallmouth are in the shallows, you can catch them by sight fishing (opposite). But when you can see the fish, they can also see you, so they're extra wary.

Because many clearwater lakes are low in nutrients, the depths contain plenty of dissolved oxygen, meaning that smallmouth can go wherever they want to find food and cover. This explains why you may find them at a depth of 30 feet or more on a calm, sunny day and in water only a few feet deep on a cloudy, windy day.

Clearwater smallmouth have another habit that often befuddles anglers. In summer and early fall, they spend a great deal of their time chasing baitfish suspended in open water. You'll sometimes see them busting into schools of baitfish on the surface over water more than 50 feet deep. Savvy anglers always stop to make a few casts when they see this kind of surface action.

In many ultra-clear lakes, the best smallmouth action starts at dusk and continues well into the night, particularly in the heat of summer. The fish become much more aggressive after dark and you can "call" them up from water as deep as 25 feet using shallow-running lures like spinnerbaits and floating minnowbaits.

Smallmouth in clear water are easily spooked. This means you must stay low, avoid throwing your shadow over the fish, use realistic lures and present them delicately.

As a rule, lures in dark or natural colors work better than those in bright or fluorescent colors. And small lures with a subtle but lifelike action generally outproduce big ones with a violent action. This explains why "split-shotting"—inching along small soft plastics or live bait with a rig consisting of only a hook and a split-shot—is so popular among clearwater anglers.

Heavy or highly visible line will greatly reduce the number of strikes from clearwater smallmouth. Be sure to use low-vis mono, either clear or green, in the lightest weight suitable for the conditions. You'll rarely need line heavier than 8-pound test, and you might want to go as light as 4-pound test.

How to Sight Fish

1 Wearing polarized sunglasses, stand in the bow of your boat and move slowly using a bow-mount trolling motor. Keep the sun at your back to minimize glare. Look for fish or any movements or shadows that could reveal their presence.

2 When you spot a smallmouth, toss a tubebait or other small soft plastic well past the fish using a low-trajectory cast. Retrieve the lure slowly so it passes no more than 3 feet in front of the fish.

Tips for Catching Clearwater Smallmouth

Carry an extra rod rigged with a tailspinner or some other lure you can cast a long distance in case you come upon surface smallmouth activity.

Look for other smallmouth following a fish you have hooked. The followers are super-aggressive and will immediately grab another lure dangled in their face by a second angler.

RIVER FISHING

The thought of fishing for smallmouth in a river, especially a big one with diverse habitat, is intimidating to anglers who spend most of their time fishing lakes. Not only do the fish relate to much different kinds of cover, their seasonal movement patterns are much different as well.

But "river rats" will tell you that it's easier to catch smallmouth in a river than a lake because moving water concentrates the fish. The secret is knowing where to look and when (pp. 48-55), and then tailoring your fishing methods to the conditions.

As a rule, river smallmouth are more aggressive than their lake-dwelling relatives. In still water, a fish has plenty of time to size up a potential food item; in moving water, it must grab its food immediately or the current will sweep it away. This means that you can use a wider selection of lures and that your presentation need not be quite as precise.

The best river fishermen have the ability to "read the water" and recognize current patterns that reveal underwater structure like boulders, gravel bars and wing dams. They also know what current speed is best for smallmouth—not too fast and not too slow.

The biggest challenge to river fishermen is the frequently changing water level. In small to medium-sized streams, low water concentrates the fish in the deepest holes, so you know right where to find them. Rising water generally draws the fish into shallower water, while falling water pushes them deeper. It's important to establish a reference point along the bank that enables you to precisely monitor the water level from day to day.

Many of the fishing techniques used by lake fishermen work equally well in rivers. But to consistently catch smallmouth in moving water, you'll have to expand your bag of tricks. Here are some methods that will greatly improve your river-fishing success:

"Slipping" the Main Channel

Point your boat directly upstream and motor forward just slightly slower than the speed of the current. This way, your boat will "slip" downstream very slowly, giving you ample time to work shoreline and in-stream structure. When you want to stop the boat to work a spot more thoroughly, just speed up a little to hold your position. Popular lures for slipping include jigs, spinners, crankbaits and minnowbaits.

Pitching a Wingdam

Check the entire wingdam to determine where the current is just right for smallmouth. The current will be fastest toward the channel end. Anchor your boat far enough upstream of the wingdam that the top of the dam is within easy casting distance. Cast a jig tipped with a curlytail or minnow onto the top of the dam and work it down the upstream lip. If you don't get a strike after a few casts, reposition your boat laterally until you find the fish.

Working a Pool

You can fish a small pool or eddy by slipping (top), but to thoroughly cover a large one, you should anchor. Although every pool is different, the active smallmouth will usually be found along the upstream lip where they have the first opportunity to grab food that drifts into the pool. The best strategy is to anchor just upstream of the pool and work the upper lip using a jig or live-bait rig.

Making a Float Trip

One of the very best ways to fish a small to medium-sized stream is to make a float trip. Using a jon boat that draws only a few inches of water, you can drift downstream over shallow shoals and riffle areas that would be impassible with a large craft.

Along the way, you can spend a few minutes fishing each likely pool, eddy or run. On a full day's float, you'll cover from 7 to 10 miles of stream.

The problem is, you may not be able to motor back upstream to your starting point without banging your propeller on the rocks. The best solution is to use two vehicles, parking one at the take-out spot and, when the trip is completed, driving back upstream to pick up the other vehicle and boat trailer.

Here's how a float trip is normally done:

1 Launch your boat at the upstream end of the reach you want to fish. Before launching, leave another vehicle at a downstream take-out site.

2 Look for likely smallmouth spots as you drift downstream. Stop long enough to work each one thoroughly.

3 Tip up your motor when drifting over shallow shoals. It's a good idea to carry a pair of oars to help maneuver the boat in shallow water.

4 Wear shorts and tennis shoes so when you come to an impassible riffle, you can jump out and pull the boat across to deeper water.

5 Continue drifting until you reach the take-out spot, then pull your boat up on the bank and drive back to get the other vehicle and trailer.

Locate wingdams and other man-made structures in large rivers using a navigation chart. Many of these structures are submerged and not obvious to the untrained eye.

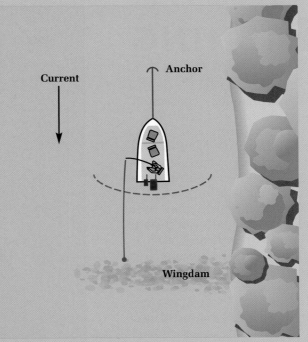

Anchor on a long rope to fish wingdams and other in-stream structure. Then, you can use your trolling motor to pull your boat to either side (dotted line), enabling you to work the structure's entire width.

Outfit your motor with a prop guard when fishing a shallow stream. This model, made of stainless steel, attaches to your lower unit and protects the skeg and bottom blade.

During the winter months, look for smallmouth around warmwater power-plant discharges. The warm water concentrates baitfish which, in turn, draws large numbers of smallmouth and other gamefish.

TROPHY FISHING

When you see a 5-pound-plus bronzeback cartwheel out of the water and then make a sizzling run back to the depths, it's easy to understand why so many anglers get hooked on fishing for trophy smallmouth.

But if catching giant smallies is your goal, you'd better plan on spending a fair amount of time researching the best locations and times, along with the techniques that are most likely to produce under the conditions.

Prime Locations

In most regions, the waters likely to produce big smallmouth are well known, so the local bait-shop operator or a knowledgeable local angler can point you in the right direction. But by recognizing the qualities of trophy smallmouth water, you might just be able to find a few gems that have yet to be discovered by the masses. Here's what you should be looking for:

• **A significant area of deep water.** The best trophy smallmouth lakes almost always have a basin at least 40 feet deep with gradually tapering rather than fast-sloping structure.

• **Big water.** As a rule, big water means big fish, and smallmouth are no exception. In fact, anglers around the country are discovering surprising numbers of big smallmouth in bays of the Great Lakes and other huge natural lakes throughout the north country. As is the case with

many other kinds of gamefish, the "fish-bowl" effect limits growth in smaller waters.

• **A relatively low smallmouth population.** In waters where smallmouth are numerous, they seldom reach trophy size because there is too much competition for the available food. Rather than selecting a body of water known for its smallmouth fishery, focus on one where

smallmouth are not a major drawing card.

• **Baitfish as the major food source.** An abundance of baitfish, particularly oily ones like shad or ciscoes, usually results in good-sized smallmouth. If crustaceans, insects or other invertebrates are the main food source, however, the fish generally grow more slowly and seldom reach trophy size.

Best Times

The very best time to catch a real trophy is during the pre-spawn period. Assuming the season is open on your favorite lake or river, start fishing about two weeks before spawning begins. The hot bite continues as long as the fish are bedding.

The odds of bagging a giant smallie are also good in fall, when the water temperature drops below 60°F. Then, the fish begin feeding heavily in preparation for winter and are tightly concentrated, usually on sharp-sloping structure. The feeding binge continues until the water temperature falls to about 45°F.

In rivers and streams, your chances of finding big smallmouth are best during the low-water periods that often occur from late summer into fall. Then, large numbers of fish concentrate in the deepest pools and eagerly attack practically any kind of lure or bait tossed their way.

During low water, stream smallmouth are drawn to easily identifiable pools.

Trophy Smallmouth the Kentucky Way

Here's how one good old boy catches big smallmouth on Kentucky's Cumberland Reservoir. To start, catch fresh bait daily—skipjack, alewife, shad, whatever forage the bass use. Remove sick or injured baitfish as the day goes on (left). Pinch on a small split-shot or two 18 inches above a fine wire hook—just enough weight to keep the bait sinking slowly and naturally—then hook a baitfish through the nostrils (middle). Cast to shore and allow the rig to sink. Rotate rods in your holders (arrows, right photo) as you mooch along the shoreline and work the various depths, placing a rod in the farthest holder after each cast. Note: Be sure to follow all regulations regarding how many lines you can fish at once.

INDEX